# Saints
# & Scoundrels
# *of the* Bible

# Saints
# & Scoundrels
## *of the* Bible

The Good, the Bad, and the Downright Dastardly

Linda Chaffee Taylor
Carol Chaffee Fielding
Drenda Thomas Richards

HOWARD BOOKS
A DIVISION OF SIMON & SCHUSTER
New York    London    Toronto    Sydney

Our purpose at Howard Books is to:
• *Increase faith* in the hearts of growing Christians
• *Inspire holiness* in the lives of believers
• *Instill hope* in the hearts of struggling people everywhere
Because He's coming again!

Published by Howard Books, a division of Simon & Schuster, Inc.
1230 Avenue of the Americas, New York, NY 10020
www.howardpublishing.com

*Saints & Scoundrels of the Bible* © 2007 The Livingstone Corporation

Library of Congress Cataloging-in-Publication Data

Saints & scoundrels of the Bible : the good, the bad, and the downright dastardly.
p.cm.
ISBN: 978-1-4165-6677-9 (tradepaper)
1. Bible—Biography. I. Title: Saints and scoundrels of the Bible.
BS571.S225 2008
200.9'2—dc22
2008006599

ISBN–13: 978-1-4165-6677-9


1   3   5   7   9   10   8   6   4   2

Manufactured in the United States of America

For information regarding special discounts for bulk purchases, please contact:
Simon & Schuster Special Sales at 1-800-456-6798 or business@simonandschuster.com.

Interior design by Davina Mock-Maniscalco

Produced with the assistance of The Livingstone Corporation (www.LivingstoneCorp.com).
Project staff includes Linda Taylor, Carol Chaffee Fielding, Drenda Thomas Richards, Betsy Schmitt, Linda Washington, Gene Smillie, Mary Horner Collins, and Will Reaves.

# Contents

# Introduction

The gossip magazines at the local grocery store have nothing on the Bible. If you want to read about people making either bad or heroic decisions, being wise or unwise in marriage, standing strong or following the crowd, being perpetrators or victims of horrible crimes, then look no further than the Bible on your shelf.

*Saints & Scoundrels of the Bible* focuses on the people of the Bible. In this little book, you'll be introduced to people in the following categories:

- "Winners and Whiners" shows you some of the winners in the Bible (like Rahab, Ruth, Esther, and Daniel) along with some of the whiners (like Miriam, Aaron, Ahab, and Jonah).
- "Big Shots and Mug Shots" focuses on some of the big shots (such as Hezekiah and Nicodemus), along with some criminal types (such as Cain and Achan) who show up in the Bible.
- In the "Leaders and Laborers" section you'll be introduced to those who led (like Abraham and Joshua) and those who labored (like Noah and Nehemiah).
- The "Prophets and Losses" section gives you a snapshot of the lives of all of the Bible's prophets. You'll find out what they said, did, and in some cases lost, in order to bring God's message to his people.

- "Freaks and Greeks" looks at some unusual people in the Bible (like Goliath and Samson) and some of the Greeks who show up in the New Testament Church (like Timothy and Titius Justus).
- Finally, "Dashers and Vixens" points out some of the people caught running in Scripture (like Jacob and David) and some of the vixens who got themselves into deep trouble (like Delilah and Jezebel).

Scripture references are provided with each profile so you can read the story for yourself. In addition, we have created "Factoid" lists for key characters to give you a quick snapshot of that person's life and where you can read about him or her.

Enjoy *Saints & Scoundrels of the Bible*. You may never have to buy another magazine!

# PART ONE

# Winners and Whiners

# Extreme Exit—
# Part 1

*Enoch Is Taken by God*

Factoids: Enoch
- *Date:* Prediluvian era
- *Occupation:* Prophet, walker with God
- *Family Ties:* Father, Jared; son, Methuselah; great-great-great-great-great grandfather, Adam
- *Mentioned in the Bible:* Genesis 5:18–19, 21–24; 1 Chronicles 1:3; Luke 3:37; Hebrews 11:5; Jude 1:14

THE LONG LISTS of names are somewhat yawn-inducing. "Adam became the father of Seth, and Seth became the father of Enosh"—yawn—"and Enosh became the father of . . ."

Keep reading this list of names in Genesis 5 and you find this eye-opening yawn stopper: "When Enoch was 65 years old, he became the father of Methuselah. After the birth of Methuselah, Enoch lived in close fellowship with God for another 300 years, and he had other sons and daughters. Enoch lived 365 years, walking in close fellowship with God. Then one day he disappeared, because God took him" (Genesis 5:21–24 NLT).

Talk about an extreme exit! What in the world happened? And then, even though we want to know more, the list goes on: "Methuselah became the father of Lamech . . ."

Now, fast-forward to the New Testament book of Hebrews. The unknown writer of Hebrews saw Enoch as more than just a name on a list, for he wrote, "It was by faith that Enoch was taken up to heaven without dying—'he disappeared, because God took him.' For before he was taken up, he was known as a person who pleased God" (Hebrews 11:5). Following that explanation of Enoch's character is the Bible's well-known definition of faith: "It is impossible to please God without faith. Anyone who wants to come to him must believe that God exists and that he rewards those who sincerely seek him" (Hebrews 11:6).

In his 365 years on this planet, Enoch carved out a reputation as a person who pleased God. The secret? Walking in close fellowship with God. Enoch was literally a walking definition of faith.

The Genesis passage tells us that Enoch had sons and daughters. He was a family man—presumably with some kind of occupation, a home, a wife and children, and probably grandchildren and great-grandchildren. He lived a life not much different from his contemporaries (and not much different from ours in some respects); yet he did it all while walking in close fellowship with God. In fact, God enjoyed it so much that he simply took Enoch to heaven. Enoch didn't have to endure illness or death. Instead, God brought Enoch into his presence. (Only one other person had that privilege—Elijah. You can read about him in "Extreme Exit—Part 2," page 21.)

What does it take to have that kind of enduring fellowship with God? The clue seems to be in the word *walking*. Walking is a step-by-step process toward a destination. Each step matters. Each step moves us forward. Each step is intentional. Each step is a choice. If we want to have close fellowship with God, we must take each "step" in our lives—each action, each choice, each decision, each thought—with the constant desire to please God. Enoch did it for 365 years. What would it take for us to do it today, tomorrow, and for the rest of our lives?

*Enoch's story is told in Genesis 5:21–24.*

# Sibling Rivalry

*Miriam and Aaron Whine About Moses's Leadership*

Factoids: Miriam
- *Domicile:* Egypt; Sinai peninsula
- *Date:* About 1400 B.C.
- *Occupation:* Prophetess, songwriter
- *Family Ties:* Brothers, Aaron and Moses
- *Mentioned in the Bible:* Exodus 2; 15; Numbers 12; 20:1; Deuteronomy 24:9; 1 Chronicles 6:3; Micah 6:4

Factoids: Aaron
- *Domicile:* Egypt; Desert of Sinai
- *Date:* About 1400 B.C.
- *Occupation:* Priest; Moses's second-in-command
- *Family Ties:* Brother, Moses; sister, Miriam; sons, Nadab, Abihu, Eleazar, Ithamar
- *Mentioned in the Bible:* Exodus 4:14–Deuteronomy 10:6; Hebrews 7:11

ASK CHILDREN WITH SIBLINGS what bugs them most, and they'll undoubtedly answer, "My little brother" or "My big sister." Sibling rivalry has been around since the dawn of mankind, when Cain got all bent out of shape because God liked Abel's offering better (see "The First Fratricide," page 39). But as brothers and sisters mature, there is less competition and strife, right?

Don't bet on it.

Well advanced in years (we're talking into their eighties or nineties), Aaron and Miriam had issues with their younger brother's leadership. To put it bluntly, they were jealous that God had chosen Moses—not either of them—to lead the Hebrew nation.

Rather than come right out and say that they were envious of Moses's position of power, they decided to beat around the bush (not the burning one) by criticizing Moses's wife. While we don't know what was said about his wife, we do know the final comment made brought out the real issue: "Has the LORD spoken only through Moses? . . . Hasn't he also spoken through us?" (Numbers 12:2 NIV).

Immediately following their whiny episode, God chose to swiftly deal with their envy and pride. In an almost "Don't make me come down there" moment, Scripture tells us, "The LORD said to Moses, Aaron, and Miriam, 'Come out to the Tent of Meeting, all three of you.' So the three of them came out" (12:4). God had had enough of their attitude. Cloaked in a pillar of cloud (his awesome glory would have been too much for them to behold), the Lord did what most parents would do: He called out the two naughty ones for a stern talking-to. When Miriam and Aaron stepped forward, God said to them, "Listen to my words: When a prophet of the LORD is among you, I reveal myself to him in visions, I speak to him in dreams. But this is not true of my servant Moses; he is faithful in all my house. With him I speak face to face, clearly and not in riddles; he sees the form of the LORD. Why then were you not afraid to speak against my servant Moses?" (12:6–8).

To paraphrase in today's mom-and-dad jargon, God basically said to the older siblings, "Look, you two, I may speak to you in visions and dreams, but Moses over there, I speak with him face-to-face. He's my golden boy—humble and faithful—my chosen leader for your people. What right have you to say anything against him?" And then Scripture tells us, "The anger of the LORD burned against them" (12:9).

When the cloud lifted, Miriam was completely covered with the

dreaded disease of leprosy. When Aaron saw her, he begged Moses
not to hold their sin against them. Moses cried to the Lord to heal
Miriam. God put her in "time-out" for seven days; then she was
healed and allowed back in the camp.

*Read the account of Miriam and Aaron's jealous episode in Numbers 12.*

# Learning
# the Hard Way

*The Israelites Whine About Entering the Promised Land*

FOLLOWING THE CROWD can have seriously negative
consequences. The Israelites were prime examples of this truth.

God's people were on the verge of entering the Promised Land
(Canaan). This was exciting stuff! They had waited eons for this
moment. Moses, their leader, was directed by God to do some re-
connaissance. He chose one man from each tribe and sent these
men as spies into Canaan. Before they embarked on the top-secret
mission, Moses asked the spies to check out some specific things: if
the land was fertile; whether the cities were fortified; how many
people lived there; if the people were strong or weak; and what the
fruit was like.

The spies were gone forty days. They traveled to every part of

Canaan before returning with souvenirs: grapes so large they had to be hoisted onto a pole and carried by two people! Ten spies gave the people of Israel some "snapshots" of their trip, saying, "We went into the land to which you sent us, and it does flow with milk and honey! Here is its fruit. But the people who live there are powerful, and the cities are fortified and very large. We even saw descendants of Anak there" (Numbers 13:27–28 NIV).

Caleb and Joshua, two of the twelve spies, were all for taking the land anyway (read about that in "Only the Lonely," page 84). But the other ten spies insisted that the people were too strong to defeat. Giving in to their fears, the Israelites whined throughout the night. And, as was their usual pattern, they complained to Moses and Aaron. "If only we had died in Egypt! Or in this desert! Why is the LORD bringing us to this land only to let us fall by the sword? Our wives and children will be taken as plunder. Wouldn't it be better for us to go back to Egypt?" (Numbers 14:2–3). Whine, whine, whine.

Now Caleb, and his fellow spy, Joshua, had heard enough. Wasn't God with them? They stepped up to the plate and insisted that God would help them defeat the people of Canaan and take the land. But the people would not listen. They wanted to stone Joshua and Caleb and go back to Egypt.

God was not happy with their response and threatened to send a plague on the people. God's anger eased when Moses pleaded for mercy. Although God forgave them, the consequences for their disbelief were severe. Because they had chosen to listen to the ten negative spies and not to Joshua and Caleb, they had to wander in the desert for forty years (one year for every day the spies were gone), until the naysayers died. Only Joshua and Caleb and the children of that generation lived to enter the Promised Land.

The people learned the hard way to trust God. But the lesson came too late.

*To read more about the whining Israelites, check out Numbers 13–14.*

# Grim Results of Grumbling

*Korah, Dathan, and Abiram Whine About Moses's Leadership*

WHAT WAS THIS, some sort of trend? It seemed that no one was happy with Moses's leadership except God (see "Sibling Rivalry," page 5). The "children of Israel" acted like . . . well, like children most of the time, and Moses spent a lot of time begging God to give them another chance.

Shortly after Israel's great rebellion against God, in which God punished them by condemning them to wander the desert for forty years, Korah decided to have his own little rebellion against Moses. It seems that he forgot that God had placed Moses in authority over him and everyone else.

Korah gathered 250 supporters to his cause and had a showdown. Korah's complaint? "You have gone too far! Everyone in Israel has been set apart by the LORD, and he is with all of us. What right do you have to act as though you are greater than anyone else among all these people of the LORD?" (Numbers 16:3 NLT). In other words, as a child might proclaim, "You're not the boss of me!"

Well, God had put Moses in charge, and Moses wasn't afraid to prove it. He also explained that the very fact that the Levites had been chosen to minister before God was not an insignificant matter.

As a Levite, Korah already had a special ministry; "Are you now demanding the priesthood as well?" Moses asked (16:10).

Perhaps that was indeed the case. Back when the Hebrews were still slaves in Egypt, they knew that the Egyptian priests were very wealthy and even held some political sway within the Pharaoh's court. Korah and his fellow Levites must have thought that Moses and Aaron were as well off as those Egyptian priests, and they wanted in on the action.

Dathan and Abiram, also Levites who took their turns assisting in the daily functions of the tabernacle, had their own warped memory of life in Egypt and their own attitude of disrespect toward Moses. When summoned to come to Moses, they replied, "We refuse to come before you! Isn't it enough that you brought us out of Egypt, a land flowing with milk and honey, to kill us here in this wilderness, and that you now treat us like your subjects?" (16:12–13). They whined that Moses hadn't led them anywhere. "Where was the Promised Land?" they demanded. (Never mind that it was the people's sin that caused their little diversion in the wilderness, and not Moses.) Basically they said, "You haven't delivered the goods, Moses. And you shouldn't be our leader. We should all be leaders. After all, we're all chosen by God."

What was Moses to do? He told them all—all of the malcontents and Aaron—to appear before the Lord the next day. At the Tent of Meeting, God's glorious presence appeared in their midst. In yet another "I'm sick of dealing with these people's whining" moment, God said to Moses and Aaron, "Get away from all these people so that I may instantly destroy them" (16:21). Moses and Aaron begged God to spare the people's lives, but God had had enough. He told Moses and Aaron to declare that everyone must move away from the tents of Korah, Dathan, and Abiram.

No sooner had the people done so when "the ground suddenly split open beneath them. The earth opened its mouth and swallowed the men. . . . They went down alive into the grave, along with all their belongings. The earth closed over them, and they all vanished from among the people of Israel" (16:31–33).

The ringleader of the rebellion, Korah, had once been a leader, but his goals were replaced by greed. Dathan and Abiram are prime examples of what happens when we lose perspective. Together these men were not content serving God, and when they tried to grab more than they deserved, they lost everything.

*To read the whole story of Korah, Dathan, and Abiram and their complaining and untimely demise, see Numbers 16.*

# A Wanton Woman Wins

*Rahab, the Prostitute, Chooses the Hebrews' God*

Factoids: Rahab
- *Domicile:* Jericho
- *Date:* Around 1400 B.C.
- *Occupation:* Prostitute, but gave that up
- *Family Ties:* Joined the Hebrews; is mentioned as an ancestor of King David and Jesus Christ (Matthew 1:5)

- *Mentioned in the Bible:* Joshua 2:1–21; 6:22–23;
  Matthew 1:5; Hebrews 11:31; James 2:25

OKAY, the first question is about those Hebrew spies . . . sent to check out the city of Jericho and they take a little side trip to a brothel? What's that about?

Well, things are not always as they appear. The text doesn't tell us all the details, but we can be fairly certain that these Hebrew men had far more important things on their minds than a night with a prostitute. Joshua had given them an extremely important task— one that almost got bungled right at the start, were it not for this courageous wanton woman.

Many strangers entered the city and made a stop at Rahab's establishment. If this was the spies' reasoning, their visit to Rahab was a strategic move because it would arouse little suspicion. In addition, her house was built into the city wall, making a quick escape possible (which, as it turned out, was just what was needed). Given the fact that the men were in the city for barely a few seconds before arousing suspicion, we can only conclude that God sent them to the home of this woman who not only would keep their secret from the king himself but also would hide them and help them escape. God knew her heart was wide open to him.

Perhaps on a day when business was slow, she had walked out on the roof of her house and thought about her life, wondering if there might be more than running a brothel. Perhaps as she listened to people talk in her establishment or around town, she heard the stories of a massive group of people on the move whose mighty God went before them and dried up seas and conquered armies. God softened her heart so that by the time the spies arrived on her doorstep, she expressed her faith in this yet unknown God, saying:

> I know that the LORD has given this land to you and that a great fear of you has fallen on us, so that all who live in this country are melting in fear because of you. We have

heard how the Lord dried up the water of the Red Sea for you when you came out of Egypt, and what you did to Sihon and Og, the two kings of the Amorites east of the Jordan, whom you completely destroyed. When we heard of it, our hearts melted and everyone's courage failed because of you, for the LORD your God is God in heaven above and on the earth below. (Joshua 2:9–11 NIV)

In that moment, she made a choice to follow this God. What it entailed, she did not yet know. She knew the city would be attacked and asked the spies to protect her home and the family she would gather there.

And so it was. After the city of Jericho fell (literally) to the Hebrew people, Joshua sent the spies into the city to bring out Rahab and her family (Joshua 6:22–23). The book of Hebrews sums it up: "By faith the prostitute Rahab, because she welcomed the spies, was not killed with those who were disobedient" (Hebrews 11:31).

How did Rahab know? The answer can only be that she called out in some need to the true God, whom she didn't know, and God answered her need, honored her request, and drew her to himself.

*Read about Rahab's courageous choice in Joshua 2.*

# Finding Faith

*Ruth Stays with Naomi and Chooses Loyalty and Faith*

Factoids: Ruth
- *Domicile:* Moab, then Bethlehem
- *Date:* Around 1200 B.C.
- *Occupation:* Wife, widow, wife again
- *Family Ties:* First husband, Kilion; mother-in-law, Naomi; second husband, Boaz. She is mentioned as the great-grandmother of King David (Ruth 4:21–22) and an ancestor of Jesus Christ (Matthew 1:5).
- *Mentioned in the Bible:* The book of Ruth; Matthew 1:5

READING THE STORY OF RUTH raises a few questions, one of which might be: Why in the world would a young, beautiful widow choose to stay with her mother-in-law instead of seeking a new husband?

After the death of her two sons, Naomi told her daughters-in-law, "Go back, each of you, to your mother's home" (Ruth 1:8 NIV). An elderly widow, she knew there was nothing she could provide—they had a better chance returning to their homes and starting over. One of the daughters-in-law, Orpah, chose to leave. But Ruth couldn't be persuaded to leave Naomi: "Don't urge me to leave you or to turn back from you. Where you go I will go, and where you stay I will stay. Your people will be my people and your God will be my God" (1:16).

What was she thinking?

They headed for Judah, a land completely foreign to Ruth.

Rather than helplessly depending on Naomi or curling up in the fetal position in despair, Ruth took upon herself the degrading task of gleaning the wheat and barley fields. After all, she and Naomi had to eat. Though the task was exhausting, Ruth worked all day, picking up what the harvesters dropped. This was a sort of ancient welfare program—Israelite law stated that dropped grain was to be left for the poor to glean (Leviticus 19:9–10; 23:22; Deuteronomy 24:19).

Imagine how Ruth must have felt. She had lost her husband, had moved to a strange land in which she knew no one except her mother-in-law, and then had to follow harvesters all day and pick up whatever they dropped, for her dinner. Someone else might have collapsed in a blubbering heap. Yet, in the midst of these hardships, she remained loyal to Naomi.

In turn Naomi formed a plan to help Ruth. One day Ruth returned from gleaning and brought home around three-fifths of a bushel of grain. She also recounted how kind Boaz had been to her. Naomi decided it was time to reward her daughter-in-law's faithfulness in the only way she could—she was going to get Ruth a new husband.

And so it came about that Ruth followed Naomi's weird ancient husband-catching advice (see Ruth 3), and Boaz took Ruth as his wife.

What turned the women's difficult situation into a time of rejoicing? It all came down to loyalty (Ruth to Naomi, Naomi to God), faithfulness, and kindness. We often look for tangible, material rewards for our good deeds or our loyalty to God, when sometimes the real blessings are right around us in our family and friends!

*Read about Ruth's faithfulness and loyalty in the book of Ruth.*

# A Fool and His Honey
# Are Soon Parted

*Abigail Defuses a Bad Situation and Gets Rid of a Bad Husband*

Factoids: Abigail
- *Domicile:* Carmel
- *Date:* Around 1025 B.C.
- *Occupation:* Homemaker
- *Family Ties:* First husband, Nabal; second husband, King David; son, Kileab
- *Mentioned in the Bible:* 1 Samuel 25; 2 Samuel 2; 1 Chronicles 3:1

WHILE THERE are many good husbands out there, some men don't deserve their wives. Nabal was one such man. We are told that Abigail "was an intelligent and beautiful woman" but her husband was "surly and mean" (1 Samuel 25:3 NIV). Basically, he was a jerk.

Nabal was a wealthy man with plenty of sheep and enough goats to feed an army and still have many left over. David wasn't being rude when he sent messengers asking Nabal to feed his six hundred men. Hospitality customs of the day dictated that travelers—especially those who helped protect the people and flocks of the land, as David and his men had been doing—were to be respected and fed. Nabal could easily have afforded to honor this custom.

But being the mean and surly guy that he was, Nabal refused to be hospitable. He insulted David and told David's messengers to take a hike. When David heard about Nabal's response, he was ticked off, to put it mildly. Actually, he told four hundred of his men, "Put on your swords" (25:13), and they marched straight for Nabal's estate.

Fortunately, a servant of the household hightailed it to Abigail and told her the whole story. Knowing that disaster would follow her husband's idiotic behavior, "Abigail lost no time" (25:18).

Without telling her husband, she and her servants loaded up the family pack mules with all kinds of edible goodies and headed out, hoping to intercept David and his men. "As she came riding her donkey into a mountain ravine, there were David and his men descending toward her, and she met them" (25:20).

Imagine David's surprise when, as he's still sputtering about Nabal's rudeness, a strange woman hops off her donkey and bows down before him, begging forgiveness for her husband's behavior! Surely he was in no mood to listen to reason, yet he could not ignore this beautiful woman (which gets him into trouble later on, but that's another story), and what must have been a long line of donkeys loaded down with food. Abigail's quick action and skillful negotiation prevented the destruction of her entire household, as well as an act of sinful vengeance by Israel's future king.

David thanked Abigail for her good judgment, accepted her gifts, and returned to his camp. She probably breathed a sigh of relief before gathering her strength once again in order to tell her husband what she had done. Although she might have feared Nabal's reaction, it turned out that any anxiety was unnecessary. When Nabal heard, he went into heart failure and became "like a stone" (25:37). Ten days later, he died.

The unfortunate Nabal is an excellent example of how a bad attitude and rash behavior can lead to a downfall.

*Read about Abigail's courage and quick thinking in 1 Samuel 25.*

# Whining over a Winery

## *Ahab Whines About Wanting Naboth's Vineyard*

Factoids: Ahab

- *Domicile:* The palace in Samaria, capital of the northern kingdom of Israel
- *Date:* Around 870 B.C.
- *Occupation:* King of the northern kingdom
- *Family Ties:* Father, Omri; wife, Jezebel; sons, Ahaziah, Joram
- *Mentioned in the Bible:* 1 Kings 16:28–22:40; 2 Chronicles 18–22; Micah 6:16

A HAB WAS IN A BAD MOOD—a *really* bad mood. And no one should mess with a king who's in a really bad mood. But perhaps it's understandable why his mood was so bleak. After all, Ahab had just been told that he was going to die because he had been disobedient. Not exactly the best news to hear. No wonder he went home "angry and sullen" (1 Kings 20:43 NLT).

So he got home, ate everything in the fridge (well, he would have if he'd had a fridge), and then sat out on his balcony. Apparently for the first time he noticed a really nice vineyard just outside the palace walls. And he decided he wanted it.

He called up the owner of the vineyard, Naboth, and had him come over. He asked Naboth if he could purchase the vineyard, or at least trade it for another one. Ahab explained that this particular vineyard was convenient to his palace, and so he felt like he was offering Naboth a fair deal. He didn't expect Naboth to turn him down.

But Naboth did.

Naboth wasn't being recalcitrant or greedy; Naboth had a very good reason for refusing to sell: "The LORD forbid that I should give you the inheritance that was passed down by my ancestors" (1 Kings 21:3). No amount of money would have been enough to change Naboth's mind. It didn't have to do with the money; it had to do with the fact that Naboth didn't want to break God's laws by allowing ancestral land to go to someone outside his family. The Lord had commanded, "None of the territorial land may pass from tribe to tribe, for all the land given to each tribe must remain within the tribe to which it was first allotted" (Numbers 36:7). The land had been in his family for generations; it wasn't for sale; thanks anyway, Mr. King. End of story.

Not so fast.

Ahab became "angry and sullen" once again (1 Kings 21:4). The guy seemed to have a pattern going on here. He crawled into bed with his face to the wall and refused to come downstairs for dinner. His wife went to check on him.

Now, Jezebel was one of those women you don't want to tangle with. She and Ahab made up what might be truly called a "gruesome twosome." When the Bible begins to give the record of Ahab's reign, it says, "As though it were not enough to follow the example of Jeroboam [another evil king], he [Ahab] married Jezebel, the daughter of King Ethbaal of the Sidonians, and he began to bow down in worship of Baal. First Ahab built a temple and an altar for Baal in Samaria. Then he set up an Asherah pole. He did more to provoke the anger of the LORD, the God of Israel, than any of the other kings of Israel before him" (16:31–33).

Jezebel was used to getting what she wanted. As the northern kingdom of Israel sank deeper into idol worship, Jezebel had gone on a search-and-destroy mission to kill off all the prophets of the Lord (see 1 Kings 18:4). When she heard that her husband was upset because the guy next door wouldn't sell him his garden, she took matters into her own hands. She threw the covers off the king and told him to get up and eat. She would get the garden for him.

And get it she did. Poor Naboth was just trying to do the right thing and obey God's laws—unfortunately, God's laws no longer meant anything to the leadership in Israel at the time. Jezebel set up a scheme, had some people lie, and made sure Naboth was murdered. She told her hubby the news, and "Ahab immediately went down to the vineyard of Naboth to claim it" (21:16).

Ahab got his garden, but he also got himself another batch of bad prophecies in the process.

*Read about Ahab, Jezebel, and Naboth in 1 Kings 21.*

# Extreme Exit—
# Part 2

*Elijah Is Taken to Heaven in a Chariot of Fire*

Factoids: Elijah
- *Domicile:* Gilead
- *Date:* Around 875 B.C.
- *Occupation:* Prophet
- *Family Ties:* None mentioned, but his contemporaries included King Ahab and Queen Jezebel, and another prophet, named Obadiah
- *Mentioned in the Bible:* 1 Kings 17–19; 21; 2 Kings 1–2; 2 Chronicles 21:12–15; Malachi 4:5–6; Matthew 11:14; 16:14; 17:3–13; 27:47–49; Luke 1:17; 4:25–26; John 1:19–25; Romans 11:2–4; James 5:17–18

E LIJAH IS PROBABLY the most famous of the prophets of Israel. He had a close, personal relationship with God, and God used him to perform miracles, including raising a child from the dead, predicting the beginning and end of a three-year drought, calling down fire from heaven, and much more. However, the part of his life that intrigues us the most is the end, but we can't call it his death, because he didn't die!

Here's how it went down. Elijah was on his way to Bethel from Gilgal, accompanied by Elisha, sort of a "junior prophet." Once they arrived in Bethel, a "company of prophets" (2 Kings 2:3 NIV) joined them. (A company of prophets was like a school of disciples of a well-known prophet.) They continued on to Jericho, and another company joined them there. Apparently they were all aware that this would be Elijah's last day on earth, as each company asked Elisha, "Do you know that the LORD is going to take your master from you today?" (2:3, 5). Their question was probably heartbreaking for Elisha, and he replied that he was aware, "but do not speak of it."

Elijah asked Elisha to stay behind. Knowing that his master would soon leave him, Elisha was eager for every last moment, word of advice, or wisdom that he could absorb from this great prophet of God. With the group of students a respectful distance away, Elijah struck the waters of the Jordan River. The waters parted, and he and Elisha crossed the river on dry ground.

Finally, Elijah asked, "Tell me, what can I do for you before I am taken from you?" (2:9). "Let me inherit a double portion of your spirit," Elisha replied (2:10). Elisha's request might seem a bit odd, but what he was really asking for was to be Elijah's successor, to continue his work as a prophet and accomplish even more for God. Only God could grant this request, but Elijah told him, "If you see me when I am taken from you, it will be yours—otherwise not" (2:10).

The next scene is one of the most amazing events of the Bible. Scripture states that a chariot of fire and horses of fire appeared. Elijah went up to heaven in a whirlwind. (He is the second person mentioned in Scripture to be taken to heaven without dying—Enoch was the first, in Genesis 5:21–24. See "Extreme Exit—Part 1," page 3.) Elisha cried out as the man whom he looked up to as a father disappeared into eternity.

The other prophets, seeing Elisha return alone and showing obvious power (the Jordan River dried up for his crossing!), asked him for permission to send out search parties, saying, "Perhaps the Spirit of the LORD has picked him up and set him down on some mountain or in some valley" (2:16). Kind of a silly thing to do since they knew in advance that Elijah would be taken from them that day!

Elisha told them not to bother, but they wouldn't take no for an answer. Fifty men searched for three days, but did not find Elijah. His extreme exit was complete. God had taken him to heaven in style.

*Read about Elijah's extreme exit in 2 Kings 2:1–18.*

# For Such a Time as This

*Esther Risks Her Life for Her People*

Factoids: Esther
- *Domicile:* The palace in Susa, capital of the Persian empire
- *Date:* Around 470 B.C.
- *Occupation:* Queen of Persia
- *Family Ties:* Husband, Xerxes (Ahasuerus); cousin, Mordecai
- *Mentioned in the Bible:* The book of Esther

THE STORY BEGINS like an ancient fairy tale. A beautiful young woman, minding her own business, finds herself at the center of a story of murder threats, intrigue, suspicion, jealousy, and conspiracy.

The story takes place about a century after the southern kingdom of Judah was overrun by the Babylonians. Many of the Jewish people were killed or taken into captivity and their nation was destroyed. Later, the Babylonians themselves were defeated by the Medo-Persians (you can read about that in Daniel 5). The Jews continued to serve God even as captives in a foreign land—first under the Babylonians, then under the Persians.

Esther (her Jewish name was Hadassah) was a young orphaned Jewish girl being raised by her cousin Mordecai in the huge Persian city of Susa (Esther 2:5–7). Mordecai was a government official under the Persian king Xerxes (some Bible versions call him Ahasuerus). Mordecai was a loyal servant of the king, even foiling an assassination plot and saving the king's life (2:21–23). After an odd series of events that included a king having a temper tantrum, a beauty pageant, and many women at a world-class spa for a full year, Mordecai's cousin Esther was chosen by the king to be his queen. A Cinderella moment for sure!

Then storm clouds began to brew. A powerful man named Haman began to have it in for Mordecai. Why? "When Haman saw that Mordecai would not bow down or show him respect, he was filled with rage. He had learned of Mordecai's nationality, so he decided it was not enough to lay hands on Mordecai alone. Instead, he looked for a way to destroy all the Jews throughout the entire empire of Xerxes" (3:5–6 NLT).

So Haman hatched a plan. As second-in-command to the king, Haman had the king's ear, and he used that to his advantage. Soon the king issued a decree that all Jews in the entire empire were to be killed the next year. As an incentive, the decree allowed that whoever killed a Jew would receive that person's property.

Think about how this would feel. Say a law is passed in your country to kill "all people under thirty" or "all people over thirty" or "all brunettes," and you are in the chosen group. You have less than a year to live, and you don't have a clue where this decision came from or why it was made in the first place. You've been minding your own business as a good citizen and now you're marked for death. No wonder "the city of Susa fell into confusion" (3:15).

Of course, the king didn't know that his beloved queen was also marked for death by this edict. She had never told him her nationality. But as his queen, she too had the king's ear. Mordecai knew this. As the details of the plot unfolded, it became clear that the only way for the Jews to be saved would be for someone to make the king see what he had done and find a way to undo it. Someone who was close to the king. That someone was Esther.

Apparently this wasn't as easy as chatting with him over breakfast. Even though she was the queen, she needed to speak to the king in his throne room to make her request. However, to go to the king without being summoned was pretty scary business. Esther was frightened at the prospect: "Anyone who appears before the king in his inner court without being invited is doomed to die unless the king holds out his gold scepter. And the king has not called me to come to him for thirty days" (4:11). For Esther to get involved meant risking her life. But Mordecai saw the situation with God's eyes. He began to see that Esther had been chosen to be queen for reasons far beyond the completion of a fairy tale: "Mordecai sent this reply to Esther: 'Don't think for a moment that because you're in the palace you will escape when all other Jews are killed. If you keep quiet at a time like this, deliverance and relief for the Jews will arise from some other place, but you and your relatives will die. Who knows if perhaps you were made queen for just such a time as this?'" (4:13–14).

And so Esther requested that the people fast and pray for three days, and even though it was against the law, she would go to see the king. "If I must die, I must die," she said bravely (4:16).

On the third day, she put on her royal robes and walked through the palace to the king's throne room. She might not make it any farther than the doorway. Her heart pounded. The previous queen had been deposed for defying this king; Xerxes was not a man to be messed with. What would he do to her? But she need not have worried. The king saw her there and extended his scepter in invitation. Esther didn't yell and scream and pound her fists; instead, she laid out a mysterious dinner plan—even inviting Haman.

In the end, Esther revealed her true identity and Haman's evil plot that had been based on his own arrogance. She pled with the king to create a new law so that her people would not be annihilated. And the king complied.

God placed this beautiful young woman where she needed to be exactly when she needed to be there. Mordecai was correct; if Esther had refused to intercede, God could have raised up someone else, for he would have protected his people. But God chose Esther, and she rose to the challenge.

*Read Esther's intriguing story in the book of Esther, specifically 4–5.*

# Woman on the Edge

*Job's Wife Whines About Her Pain*

IMAGINE BEING MARRIED to the richest man in the country. Everyone knows who he is and admires him. He is known for his integrity. Then imagine that on one very bad, awful, horrible day every piece of property you own is destroyed, all of your children are killed, and all of your businesses are burned to the ground, the records and backup gone forever. In addition, your Mercedes, Bentley, and Ferrari are totaled, your pets die, and your husband breaks out in some serious boils and blisters that he constantly scratches.

It's a sensational story. Members of the media camp out on your street, trying to memorialize your downward spiral. Friends are calling and asking questions and offering advice. What would you do? What would you say? How would you respond?

That happened to Job's wife—all of it. She responded by saying to her husband, "Do you still hold fast to your integrity? Curse God and die!" (Job 2:9 NKJV).

Why would she say such a thing? It's easy for us, in our comfortable armchairs, reading this ancient story, to wonder. But in the middle of her horrendous pain, she probably felt that God had cursed *them*. Perhaps she never had a relationship with God as her husband did. Or perhaps she spoke out of agony, without really meaning what she said.

All we know is that her pain must have been intense. While the rest of the book tells us what's going on with Job and his friends, his wife is not mentioned again. Was she in a back room of her home with the shades drawn, crying her eyes out? What did the future hold for them? Right then, the man who was her husband and provider was scratching himself like a dog with a serious flea problem—not a picture of security or sanity. Her children were gone. She'd never be a grandmother. In one moment all that made her life worth living had been whisked away from her.

Job was going through the same thing as his wife, but he never cursed God. He questioned God. He and his friends came up with some crazy ideas about why these tragedies occurred. But Job never blamed God. Job 2:10 says that "Job did not sin with his lips," and God blessed Job for that.

Grief is a painful place. In grief, it's okay to lash out and say how we feel. God is big enough to take it. But we must not stay in that place. Suffering is a part of life. Psalm 34:19 says, "Many are the afflictions of the righteous, but the LORD delivers him out of them all."

When going through trials or tragedies, we can be honest about our anger, frustration, and questions, but we must remember we are on the edge. Will it be the edge of giving up or the edge of a breakthrough? It is our choice.

*To read about Job's wife, see Job 2:9.*

# The Lion Sleeps Tonight

*Daniel's Faithfulness to God Earns Him a Place in a Den of Lions*

PERHAPS THE CHORUS of "The Lion Sleeps Tonight," based on an African legend, is going through your mind right now, especially the plaintive "Wimoweh" part of the chorus. But Daniel could have sung a different tune about lions—one that described his own real-life adventure.

Who was Daniel? The prophetic book of Daniel in the Old Testament provides a bit of his biography. He lived during the time of Israel's exile and was a survivor among many of his conquered race, forced to live in Babylon. But cream always rises to the top. Daniel was one of a number of cream-of-the-crop Israelites who became leaders in the government of Babylon.

Even a conquering nation can be conquered. When the Medes and the Persians established their empire over Babylon, the now elderly Daniel was still considered a valuable asset. King Darius appointed him one of three leaders in charge of all the other leaders—called satraps—in the kingdom.

Power often inspires envy in others. Envious men who craved Daniel's authority sought to get rid of Daniel. But his good behavior didn't provide enough ammunition to use against him at first. Banding together, the envious leaders went to the king to make a suggestion: The king should establish a law stating that anyone who prayed to any god other than the king for thirty days would be thrown into a den of hungry lions.

Why was this suggestion made? Daniel prayed to the God of Israel three times a day. It was the perfect plan to get rid of him.

Although the king made the decree, Daniel continued his prayer habit. In fact, he knelt at his window for anyone to see. And he was seen by his enemies. Thinking they had him now, the satrap-plotters went to the king with a tale of Daniel's flagrant disobedience of the decree. They reminded the king, who hesitated to carry out the law, that the law could not be changed.

The king had no choice but to have Daniel thrown into a den of lions. Unlike Nebuchadnezzar, who angrily demanded that Daniel's friends—Shadrach, Meshach, and Abednego—be put to death for their faithfulness to God, Darius actually expressed the hope that Daniel be rescued. Imagine what goes through the mind of a man who just condemned an innocent man to death. Darius could not be soothed by entertainment. His nagging conscience raged at him.

On the following morning, he went to the lions' den, his expressed hope still at the forefront of his mind. Imagine his wonder when, after calling for Daniel, he heard Daniel's voice speaking from the lions' den! God spared Daniel's life as a testament to Dan-

iel's faithfulness, while the envious men and their families found
only death in the lions' den.

*Daniel's experience in the lions' den can be found in Daniel 6.*

# An Unjust Jonah

*Jonah Whines When the Plant Wilts and Nineveh Isn't
Destroyed*

Factoids: Jonah
- *Domicile:* Joppa
- *Date:* About 785 B.C.
- *Occupation:* Prophet sent to Nineveh
- *Family Ties:* Father, Amittai
- *Mentioned in the Bible:* 2 Kings 14:25; the book of
  Jonah; Matthew 12:38–41; Luke 11:29–32

JONAH SEEMS TO BE one of those guys who just didn't get it.
    The book of Jonah tells how the prophet ignored God's com-
mand to preach repentance to the people of Nineveh and how he
was swallowed by a great fish (and later puked onto shore) as punishment.

    Jonah had no desire to go to Nineveh—perhaps he was even
afraid for his life. The people of Nineveh, the capital city of Assyria,
were known to be powerful and heartlessly cruel. This evil empire

was Israel's most dreaded enemy, so it's not surprising that Jonah wanted nothing to do with the Ninevites, much less extend to them an opportunity to repent and receive God's mercy.

But wasn't that his job? When God says go, well, the person should go! And Jonah went—but in the opposite direction.

No one deserved God's blessing less than the people of Nineveh. Jonah didn't want to bring God's message to them, for he knew that God would forgive them and extend his grace and forgiveness if the people would turn from their sin and worship him. So Jonah thought he could run away from God.

Bad idea. God found an unusual way to transport Jonah back to where he had started.

Fresh from the fish's belly, Jonah finally obeyed his calling. He went to Nineveh and preached God's message. The response was so strong that everyone—from the lowest citizen all the way up to the king himself—repented. (Read more in "A Fish Tale," page 154.)

But Jonah hadn't wanted to succeed. Instead of rejoicing that an entire city had turned from its wicked ways, Jonah had himself a pity party. Jonah believed that those in Nineveh were unworthy. When God withdrew his impending destruction, Jonah "was greatly displeased and became angry" (Jonah 4:1 NIV). He sulked and complained, saying, "O LORD, is this not what I said when I was still at home? That is why I was so quick to flee to Tarshish. I knew that you are a gracious and compassionate God, slow to anger and abounding in love, a God who relents from sending calamity. Now, O LORD, take away my life, for it is better for me to die than to live" (4:2–3).

That was why he ran away in the first place—he wanted to see God's wrath poured out on those sinners, not God's mercy! And if God was going to be merciful, well, then Jonah would rather die than see that happen.

God confronted Jonah's self-centeredness with an object lesson. First he caused a vine to quickly grow and provide shade for Jonah in the sweltering desert heat. That made Jonah happy. But the next morning, God caused a worm to chew on the vine so that it withered. God followed that up with scorching wind and a blazing sun. That made Jonah so unhappy he wanted to die.

So God asked Jonah what he was so upset about. When Jonah said he was angry that the vine had died, God told him he had no right to be mad, saying, "You have been concerned about this vine, though you did not tend it or make it grow. . . . Nineveh has more than a hundred and twenty thousand people. . . . Should I not be concerned about that city?" (4:10–11).

God's mercy is for everyone—no one is beyond his redemption. In this small book of the Bible, God spared an entire city because they repented. And Jonah, the reluctant prophet, was successful in spite of himself.

Let's hope that Jonah eventually got it.

*To read all about Jonah's whining, read Jonah 4.*

# Hunt for the Magi

## *The Magi Escape Herod's Clutches*

AT CHRISTMASTIME many programs belt out a chorus or two of "We Three Kings," the carol describing how the Magi (also known as the wise men) followed a star to find the Savior. But that carol doesn't cover the narrow escape they made at the time. How narrow an escape? Judge for yourself.

The Magi—a group of astrologers from the east (perhaps Persia)—noted a new star in the sky, which was the usual sign that a king or a conqueror had been born. Regardless of whether this "heavenly body" was a star, a planet, or a comet, the fact remains that these men saw something unusual in the sky and decided to find the one whose birth it signaled.

No one really knows whether there were three Magi or more than three. Their wanderings took them to Jerusalem, practically into the lap of King Herod. They told the king of their search for a newborn king of the Jews.

Now, there's nothing more disturbing to a power-hungry ruler than to be told that a new king has been born. The Magi's unassuming announcement didn't inspire Herod to run out and purchase a congratulations card to send on to Mary and Joseph. Instead, he asked his advisers what the news meant.

Hundreds of years before Herod's time, the prophet Micah predicted that the Messiah—the Savior promised even as far back as the Garden of Eden—would be born in Bethlehem. Herod's advisers quoted the passage from Micah: "But you, O Bethlehem Ephrathah, are only a small village among all the people of Judah. Yet a ruler of Israel will come from you, one whose origins are from the distant past" (Micah 5:2 NLT; see also Matthew 2:6).

Herod decided to send the Magi to Bethlehem to locate the king, so "I can go and worship him, too!" (Matthew 2:8). Yeah, right. They were to report back to him afterward. This is similar to stories in which the unsuspecting friend of the hero is tricked into revealing the location of the hero to the villain, isn't it? You can almost feel the noose of the trap tightening as the Magi go on their way.

By that point, Jesus was no longer a bouncing baby but a toddler living in a house with his parents. Regardless of his size, he was still a king in the eyes of the wise men. They presented gifts appropriate for a king: gold, frankincense, and myrrh. And God had a plan for protecting his son and the wise men against the wrath of

Herod. He warned them through a dream to escape to their country via a different route, instead of returning to Herod.

You have only to read the next story to see how Herod reacted to the disappearance of the wise men. In the words of Snidely Whiplash, an old-time villain, Herod's sentiment probably was, "Curses! Foiled again!"

*Read all about the Magi's great escape in Matthew 2:1–12.*

# The Whole Truth

*Apollos Learns the Full Gospel Message*

Factoids: Apollos
- *Domicile:* Alexandria, Egypt
- *Date:* Around A.D. 50
- *Occupation:* Traveling preacher
- *Family Ties:* None mentioned, but his contemporaries were Paul, Priscilla, and Aquila
- *Mentioned in the Bible:* Acts 18:24–28, 19:1; 1 Corinthians 1:12; 3:4–6, 21–22; 4:6; 16:12; Titus 3:13

IF YOU'VE EVER missed the last fifteen minutes of a movie or misplaced a book before you read the last chapter, you understand the dilemma that Priscilla and Aquila initially had with a zealous preacher named Apollos. "Meanwhile a Jew named Apollos, a native of Alexandria, came to Ephesus. He was a learned man, with a thorough knowledge of the Scriptures. He had been instructed in the way of the Lord, and he spoke with great fervor and taught about Jesus accurately, though he knew only the baptism of John. He began to speak boldly in the synagogue" (Acts 18:24–26 NIV).

Some people have an amazing ability to hold the attention of a crowd. It's even better when they have a great message to go along with it! When Apollos stepped into the scene in Ephesus, Paul had just left for other parts of Asia Minor. Filling the gap left by the amazing apostle, Apollos had a great message and great delivery; unfortunately, he didn't have the whole story. Although he was an intelligent man, capable of debating opponents of Christianity forcefully and effectively, he "knew only the baptism of John" (18:25). His preaching was based upon his vast knowledge of the Old Testament and what he knew of the teaching of John the Baptist.

His abilities caught the attention of Priscilla and Aquila, who quickly realized he was missing the last chapter of the story of Jesus. Picture Apollos there in the synagogue, pounding the podium, urging people to repent as he mightily proclaimed that the Messiah would be coming soon—having no clue that the Messiah had already come, died, been resurrected, ascended, and sent the Holy Spirit!

Being so well versed in the Old Testament prophecy of the coming Messiah, Apollos must have been floored when Priscilla and Aquila brought him up to date. What joy, what energy must have coursed through his veins as he realized the prophecies had been fulfilled. Everything the prophets foretold had already come true!

Although he could have been prideful in his natural public-speaking abilities, he was willing to listen and learn. He did not hesitate to be the student, and as a result, he became a better teacher. When he left Ephesus and arrived in Achaia, "he was a great help to those who by grace had believed" (Acts 18:27 NIV).

*Read about Apollos's teaching—and further education—in Acts 18:24–28.*

# Big Shots and Mug Shots

# The First Fratricide

*Cain Murders His Brother, Abel*

Factoids: Cain
- *Domicile:* Outside Eden, probably in present-day Iraq
- *Occupation:* Farmer
- *Family Ties:* Father, Adam; mother, Eve; brothers, Abel, Seth, and others
- *Mentioned in the Bible:* Genesis 4:1–17; Hebrews 11:4; 1 John 3:12; Jude 11

Factoids: Abel
- *Domicile:* Outside Eden, probably in present-day Iraq
- *Occupation:* Shepherd
- *Family Ties:* Father, Adam; mother, Eve; brothers, Cain, Seth, and others born after his death
- *Mentioned in the Bible:* Genesis 4:1–8; Matthew 23:35; Luke 11:51; Hebrews 11:4; 12:24; 1 John 3:12

SIBLING RIVALRY has existed since . . . well . . . since time began. The story of these first two brothers born to the first married couple offers a heartbreaking picture of the devastation of sin.

Expelled from the lush Garden of Eden because of their blatant disobedience of God, Adam and Eve settled somewhere in harsher surroundings and worked hard, struggling just to survive. Into this environment came children, two boys—first Cain, then Abel. Eve surely watched with dismay as she saw evidence of sinfulness in her children's hearts and lives.

Adam and Eve didn't have parents, and they had never been parents before. No parenting books and talk-show experts back then. They didn't have a clue how to parent. But they knew right from wrong. Like any modern-day parents, they tried to train their boys in how to act and treat each other. Perhaps Cain often found himself in the corner of the tent, sitting on a blanket in an ancient "time-out." Or maybe he was given extra chores out in the field when he was disobedient. In any case, these first parents had their hands full, for Cain probably had a rebellious streak right from the start.

In the course of life, Adam and Eve taught their children about God. They may have told Cain and Abel bedtime stories about the God who had walked in the garden with them in the cool of the evening, the God who cared for their every need, the God whom they had disobeyed. They also knew that, while they'd lost something very special, they had not been abandoned by God. And so, this little family worshipped as best they knew how, by bringing offerings to God.

The story in Genesis 4 describes both sons bringing offerings to God from their livelihood—Abel's from the flock; Cain's from the field. "The LORD looked with favor on Abel and his offering, but on Cain and his offering he did not look with favor" (Genesis 4:4–5 NIV).

Why was God not pleased with Cain's offering? The Bible doesn't tell us explicitly. As Cain pouted angrily about how God didn't like his offering, God said that if he would just "do what is right," his offering would be "accepted" (4:7). So whatever Cain was doing was wrong, he knew it, and he could have made it right.

But Cain didn't want to.

Instead, he made plans to murder his brother.

Something was definitely amiss in the psyche of this firstborn son. And perhaps there lies the answer. It may not have been simply an issue of fruit versus fat; instead, it may have been that Cain had an attitude of rebellion that displeased God. Cain knew he was to bring an animal, but he brought grain instead. He didn't care what God wanted him to do; he would do what *he* wanted. In short, he was missing a key ingredient in the lives of any who please God: faith.

The book of Hebrews offers another clue: "By faith Abel offered God a better sacrifice than Cain did. By faith he was commended as a righteous man, when God spoke well of his offerings. And by faith he still speaks, even though he is dead" (Hebrews 11:4). And the apostle John wrote, "Do not be like Cain, who belonged to the evil one and murdered his brother. And why did he murder him? Because his own actions were evil and his brother's were righteous" (1 John 3:12).

Sin had so infected this very first child that not only did Cain know what was right and refuse to do it, he also took his anger out on his younger brother by killing him. Abel had been infected by sin as well, but he had discovered faith in God and sought to please him.

In the end, only Abel was "able" to please God.

*Read about the first murder in Genesis 4:1–17.*

## FAMOUS SIBLINGS OF THE BIBLE

| SIBLINGS | REFERENCES |
|---|---|
| Cain and Abel | Genesis 4:1–16 |
| Jacob and Esau | Genesis 25:19–34; 27:1–45; 32:3–33:20 |
| The children of Jacob | Genesis 29:31–30:24; 35:16–26; 48–49 |
| Moses, Aaron, and Miriam | Exodus 2:1–4; 4:14–17; 5:27–15:20; Numbers 12 |
| Absalom, Amnon, and Tamar | 2 Samuel 13 |
| Solomon and Adonijah | 1 Kings 1:5–53, 2:13–25 |

| SIBLINGS | REFERENCES |
|---|---|
| James and John | Matthew 4:21–22; Mark 10:35–45; Luke 9:51–56 |
| Mary, Martha, and Lazarus | Luke 10:38–42; John 11:1–12:3 |
| Andrew and Peter | John 1:35–42 |
| Jesus and his brothers | John 7:1–9 |

# Achin' Achan

### Achan's Greed Causes Him to Lose Everything

EVER THINK that a little compromise here or there won't hurt anything? Well, just ask Achan about that.

Joshua and the Israelites were still reveling in their victory at Jericho. God was definitely on their side. They felt invincible. Ai was the next city on the conquering tour of Canaan. It was a small town and would be easy to take, according to the spies Joshua sent. So only three thousand soldiers were sent to conquer Ai.

Piece of cake.

But then the unexpected happened. The people of Ai chased Joshua's soldiers out of town and even killed some of them!

How could the people of an invincible God be defeated? To answer that question, we have to return to God's command to the people before Jericho fell. He had made it clear: "The city and all that is in it are to be devoted to the LORD" (Joshua 6:17 NIV). All of the gold and silver in the city of Jericho was to be set aside for the Lord's treasury. The Israelites were not to take anything for themselves.

But even though they had crumbled the walls of Jericho, something was wrong. That was obvious when the soldiers were easily defeated at Ai. Joshua cried out to God for answers. He didn't whine; instead he expressed genuine sorrow and amazement over the defeat. What would the people of Canaan think of the Israelites and their God now?

The Lord responded, "Israel has sinned. . . . They have taken some of what was set apart. They have stolen, deceived, and put [the things] with their own belongings. This is why the Israelites cannot stand against their enemies" (Joshua 7:11–12 HCSB).

There was only one thing left to do: confront the one who had stolen and deceived.

Early the next morning the people of Israel assembled according to their family groups. God told Joshua to single out the tribe of Judah. God narrowed down the clans to one clan, then to one family, then to one family member—Achan.

Joshua said, "I urge you, tell me what you have done. Don't hide anything from me" (7:19).

At that moment everyone learned that some compromises can be fatal. A robe from Babylon, a bar of gold, and two hundred shekels of silver—these were the items looted by Achan from Jericho and hidden within his tent. He learned the hard way that nothing could be hidden from God.

Joshua sent men to Achan's tent to find the items. Joshua turned to Achan and said, "Why have you troubled us? Today the LORD will trouble you!" (7:25). Achan, the stolen items, his sons, his daughters, and everything Achan owned were taken to a place later known as the Valley of Achor. (*Achor* means "trouble" for a very good reason.) Achan and his family were stoned, and all his belongings were burned. His compromise had terrible consequences for his family and for Israel. Partial obedience is still disobedience in God's eyes.

*To read more about Achan, see Joshua 7.*

# Quest for Fire

*Nadab and Abihu Die After Offering Unauthorized Fire to God*

IT MUST HAVE BEEN spectacular to watch. Aaron went through his priestly paces, offering the very first sacrifices that God had precisely prescribed. His sons Nadab and Abihu were close at hand, participating in the secondary functions, bringing the blood of the freshly slaughtered sacred animals to their father so he could sprinkle it on the holy instruments. They watched as he took the large pieces of cut-up animals and burned them on the altar. Finally, when all had been completed according to the divine instructions, Moses and Aaron withdrew into the holy tabernacle.

After a while, they appeared at the doorway, and this time the glory of God was upon them. Moses and Aaron raised their hands together and blessed all the people, and the glory of God blazed forth. The holy fire from God suddenly poured forth and utterly consumed the sacrifices that were laid upon the altar, the fat sizzling up in a loud crackling roar like a thousand Chinese firecrackers going off at once. The scene was so precious and holy that the whole nation shouted out with admiration and awe, and then fell on their faces.

Scene change: sometime later, when Aaron's sons are in the tabernacle.

Nadab and Abihu were busy preparing things. They put coals of fire in their incense burners, and then sprinkled incense over the fire. Not a good idea, guys. The Bible tells us, "In this way, they disobeyed the LORD by burning before him the wrong kind of fire, different than he had commanded. So fire blazed forth from the LORD's presence and burned them up" (Leviticus 10:1–2 NLT).

Whoa! What would you think if your pastor was suddenly burned to a crisp right there on the altar one Sunday morning? What in the world happened?

Nadab and Abihu were in positions of responsibility—whether or not they sought them. As sons of the high priest, as Levites, they had been chosen by God to be in his service. In fact, Nadab and Abihu had experienced the awesome presence of God. A little-remembered passage in Exodus says: "Then Moses, Aaron, Nadab, Abihu, and the seventy elders of Israel climbed up the mountain again. There they saw the God of Israel. Under his feet there seemed to be a surface of brilliant blue lapis lazuli, as clear as the sky itself. And though these nobles of Israel gazed upon God, he did not destroy them. In fact, they ate a covenant meal, eating and drinking in his presence!" (Exodus 24:9–11).

Nadab and Abihu had dined with God! But, for some reason, when it came to carrying out their duties as his priests, they didn't care so much about the details. Maybe they wished for other jobs. Or maybe they just had bad attitudes.

God expected better; he had a right to. So when these guys who had dined with him dared to play lightly with the rules for the sacrifices, God boiled over in holy wrath. Fire leapt out from his presence and consumed the two young priests right where they stood.

Then, as if to underline that the holiness of God must supersede even a father's grief, Aaron was instructed to keep a straight face and not mourn his loss.

With the deaths of these two young priests, God made it clear that there was no room for toying with the rules—it was too important to do things God's way.

*To read about this sad incident, see Leviticus 9:1–10:7.*

# She Nailed It

*Jael Kills Sisera and Fulfills Deborah's Prophecy*

Factoids: Jael
- *Domicile:* Likely Jericho, a city east of Jerusalem and near the Jordan River (since that is where the Kenites were from)
- *Occupation:* Housewife
- *Family Ties:* Husband, Heber the Kenite
- *Mentioned in the Bible:* Judges 4:17–18, 21–22; 5:6; 24

SOMETIMES THE MOST unlikely person winds up being the hero—or, in this case, the heroine—of a story.

During the time in Israel's history when judges led the people, the Israelites had a rocky, roller-coaster pattern of continual disobedience, repentance, and God's deliverance; disobedience, repentance, deliverance; and so on. Well, one of the times that they did evil in the sight of the Lord, God allowed a cruel oppressor named King Jabin to rule over them for twenty years. When the Israelites cried out to God for help, he gave Deborah, the current judge, the go-ahead to get the deliverance ball rolling.

In a time when women were second-class citizens, Deborah's being the judge was unusual. Deborah, who was also a prophetess, advised Barak to assemble and lead ten thousand men into battle against Jabin's army, which was led by the formidable Sisera. Barak agreed to go, but only if Deborah went with him. Deborah responded, "Of course I'll go with you. But understand that with an attitude like that, there'll be no glory in it for you. GOD will use a woman's hand to take care of Sisera" (Judges 4:9 MSG).

Deborah and Barak headed out to face Sisera and his impressive force, which included nine hundred chariots. But thanks to the Lord, Barak and his army chased Sisera's soldiers and killed every one of them—all, that is, except Sisera. He jumped out of his chariot and ran for his life, frantically searching for a place to hide. Imagine his relief at finding the tent of a woman named Jael, whose husband had shown allegiance to King Jabin. Who would ever think to find him there? Little did Sisera know, Jael did not share her husband's sentiments.

Jael invited Sisera into the tent, covered him with a blanket, and even provided milk for him to drink. Very hospitable. But then Jael did something very inhospitable. While Sisera slept, she grabbed a tent peg and hammered it into Sisera's head. Needless to say, he was soon as dead as a doornail.

When Barak came looking for Sisera, Jael showed him her handiwork: there was Sisera dead on the ground. Deborah's prophetic words had come true. God used a woman to defeat the enemy! Deborah and Barak couldn't help but sing in praise of the Lord and of Jael's courage.

Guess you could say that Jael nailed that victory.

*To read more about Jael, see Judges 4:17–24.*

# Curse for a King

## Shimei Curses King David

SOME PEOPLE JUST don't know when to keep quiet. Shimei could have used a lesson in being politically astute. Shouting down curses on the king of your country would be rule number one under what *not* to do.

King David was in a tough situation. His own son Absalom had incited a national rebellion against him. His own son! Handsome Absalom used the power of his position and, yes, his good looks to slowly build a conspiracy to take the throne from his father. The Bible says, "Absalom was greatly praised for his handsome appearance. No man in Israel was as handsome as he. No blemish was on him from his head to his foot" (2 Samuel 14:25 NCV). As the rebellion against David grew, David realized that he needed to get out of the city or bloodshed would ensue. So the king and his household—advisers, servants, wives—and various and sundry other people fled the city.

It was like a death march. "David went up the Mount of Olives, crying as he went. He covered his head and went barefoot. All the people with David covered their heads also and cried as they went" (15:30). All the people wondered what would happen to their beloved king. They feared for his life and for their lives. Surely David wondered too. What was God doing?

Then, to add insult to injury, a voice echoed across the valley as stones pelted down on David's head. Shimei had a beef with King David and saw this as the perfect opportunity to say his piece. "Get out, get out, you murderer, you troublemaker. The

LORD is punishing you for the people in Saul's family you killed! You took Saul's place as king, but now the LORD has given the kingdom to your son Absalom! Now you are ruined because you are a murderer!" (16:7–8).

But David was in such a state of sorrow and depression that he didn't even care about the insults that rained down with the stones. He allowed the cursing to continue. He figured maybe God wanted it that way—maybe Shimei was speaking the truth. So as David and his retinue marched along, Shimei ran along the ridge above them, cursing David and throwing stones and dirt as he went. End of scene.

Fast forward: Absalom's rebellion was thwarted. Absalom was killed. King David returned to Jerusalem to reclaim his throne.

And who should meet him on his march back to the city? That's right, Shimei.

But this time Shimei was singing a different tune. Surely he knew that his actions had put him in the crosshairs as an enemy of the king. And with the king back in power, well, that was going to put Shimei in a tough spot. So he ate some humble pie and apologized to the king: "Shimei son of Gera came to him and bowed facedown on the ground in front of the king. He said to the king, 'My master, don't hold me guilty. Don't remember the wrong I did when you left Jerusalem! Don't hold it against me. I know I have sinned'" (19:18–20).

How sweet.

Shimei dodged the bullet for the time being, but kings have long memories—especially for those who commit treasonous acts such as that. As King David lay dying, he gave some instructions to his son Solomon who would succeed him: "Remember, Shimei son of Gera, the Benjaminite, is here with you. He cursed me the day I went to Mahanaim. But when he came down to meet me at the Jordan River, I promised him before the LORD, 'Shimei, I will not kill you.' But you should not leave him unpunished. You are a wise man, and you will know what to do to him, but you must be sure he is killed" (1 Kings 2:8–9).

David knew that some people just don't learn their lesson. As he sought to secure a peaceful kingdom for his son, he wanted his son to know of potential enemies. Shimei stood out in David's mind and so he issued the warning. In the end, Shimei proved to be untrustworthy and Solomon had him put to death.

Shimei should have just kept his mouth shut.

*Read about Shimei in 2 Samuel 16:5–14 and 19:9–23.*

# North versus South

*The Two King "Boam's" (Reho- and Jero-) Ruin Their Respective Nations*

IT SHOULDN'T HAVE BEEN this way. King David had built a strong and powerful nation. Israel was a force to be reckoned with. The nation could have stayed strong.

But it didn't stay that way. David turned the kingdom over to his son Solomon, who started well but eventually turned away from God as he headed down the path of idol worship. At that point God promised that the kingdom would be divided and David's line would be left with only two of the twelve tribes; the remaining ten tribes would be taken away and given to Jeroboam. God told Jeroboam: "If you will listen to all that I command you, and will walk in my ways, and do what is right in my eyes by keeping my statutes and my commandments, as David my servant did, I will be with you and will build you a sure house, as I built for David, and I will give Israel to you" (1 Kings 11:38 ESV). (You can read about that in "A 'Tear'-ible Thing" on page 125.)

Solomon even got wind of this and tried to kill Jeroboam, but Jeroboam fled to Egypt and hung out there until Solomon died.

After Solomon's death, his son Rehoboam went to Shechem to be crowned king. Jeroboam hightailed it back from Egypt and led a contingent of people to speak to the young king. They asked Rehoboam if he would lighten the great load that Solomon had placed on the people (a heavy tax burden being just one of the issues). Rehoboam conferred with his father's advisers, who suggested that he follow what the people requested and lighten their burdens. Then Rehoboam talked to his buddies, and they said, "Ha! Show the people who's boss—tell them you're going to make things even worse than they were under your father."

Rehoboam thought that his friends' advice was better than the elders' advice, so he said to the people, "My father made your yoke heavy, but I will add to your yoke. My father disciplined you with whips, but I will discipline you with scorpions" (1 Kings 12:14).

Not exactly what the people wanted to hear. And rebellion ensued. "It was a turn of affairs brought about by the LORD that he might fulfill his word, which the LORD spoke by Ahijah the Shilonite to Jeroboam the son of Nebat" (12:15).

Ten tribes refused to have Rehoboam as their king, and he fled back to Jerusalem, where he maintained rule over only two tribes—Judah and Benjamin, which came to be called the southern kingdom of Judah. Jeroboam was made king over the other ten tribes, which came to be called the northern kingdom of Israel.

Problem was, Jeroboam didn't follow after God. He decided that he didn't want his people in the north having to travel into "enemy territory" to go to the temple in Jerusalem in order to worship. So he made two golden calves, setting one up in Bethel and one in Dan—that is, in the northern and southern parts of his kingdom, making it convenient for the people to worship. He said, "Behold your gods, O Israel, who brought you up out of the land of Egypt" (12:28).

And the northern kingdom spiraled downward from there. For the next few centuries, kings came and went, but not one of them sought after God or followed him. God sent many prophets to the people, but no one ever listened to them. Eventually the nation was taken into captivity by the Assyrian empire in 722 B.C.

Meanwhile, the southern kingdom had both good and bad kings. A bad king would set up idols, then a good king would arise and tear down the idols and return the people to God. Then a bad king would arise and start the cycle over. Again, prophets came to the nation to warn of impending destruction. The southern kingdom was taken into captivity in Babylon in 586 B.C.

And it didn't have to be that way. All God had asked for was obedience.

*Read about the tragic division of Israel in 1 Kings 11–12.*

# The Siege

*King Hezekiah of the Tiny Nation of Judah versus King Sennacherib of the Assyrian Empire (Place Your Bets)*

Factoids: Hezekiah
- *Domicile:* Jerusalem, capital city of the southern kingdom of Judah
- *Date:* Became king around 715 B.C. and ruled for twenty-nine years

- *Occupation:* King of Judah
- *Family Ties:* Father, Ahaz; mother, Abijah; son, Manasseh
- *Mentioned in the Bible:* 2 Kings 16:20–20:21; 2 Chronicles 28:27–32:33; Proverbs 25:1; Isaiah 1:1; 36:1–39:8; Jeremiah 15:4; 26:18–19; Hosea 1:1; Micah 1:1

S OMETIMES IT PAYS to bet on the little guy. He might look small but pack a powerful wallop. He might seem scrawny but have a black belt in karate. You never know what power lurks behind someone's seemingly powerless façade.

King Sennacherib was a big bully, and Judah was the scrawny kid on the world's playground. The powerful Assyrian empire had already invaded the northern kingdom of Israel three times (see 2 Kings 15:19–20, 15:29, and 17:1–23). The first two times, the Assyrian king Tiglath-pileser had exacted tribute and deported people. The third time, in 722 B.C., King Shalmaneser captured the capital city of Samaria, destroyed the northern kingdom, and took the people into exile. The northern kingdom ceased to exist.

All of that occurred in Hezekiah's sixth year as king of the southern kingdom of Judah (2 Kings 18:10). The Bible describes Hezekiah in this way: "He trusted in the LORD the God of Israel, so that there was none like him among all the kings of Judah after him, nor among those who were before him. For he held fast to the LORD. He did not depart from following him, but kept the commandments that the LORD commanded Moses. And the LORD was with him; wherever he went out, he prospered. He rebelled against the king of Assyria and would not serve him" (18:5–7 ESV).

Did you catch that last line? He rebelled against the king of Assyria? Talk about spitting in the bully's eye! Wasn't that just asking for trouble?

Well, yeah.

But apparently Shalmaneser didn't want to bother with the little nation by the sea. However, when King Sennacherib came to power, in Hezekiah's fourteenth year, things got ugly. Sennacherib attacked and captured several of Judah's fortified cities and Hezekiah backed down. He offered to pay the tribute, even to the point of plundering the temple for the needed silver and gold. But it was too little too late.

Sennacherib was on a roll and he wasn't going to let this back-water king defy him. He had nations to conquer! He sent his commanders to Jerusalem with a message that basically said, "Why would you trust in your God? You've been removing all of his high places and altars"—wrong, but we can cut the heathen king some slack—"and so he's probably mad at you anyway. He isn't going to help. And you know why? Because he told me to march against you and destroy you!" (Yeah, he really said this. See 2 Kings 18:25.)

The Assyrian commanders went on to tell all the people huddled inside the city in fear that they shouldn't listen to Hezekiah, that he was misleading them, yada yada. After all, no other god from any other city across the known world had been able to stop Assyria's advance. What made this little country think *their* God would be any more powerful? And what made Hezekiah think he was going to withstand the invasion?

Well, Hezekiah had a black belt . . . so to speak. Hezekiah went straight to God. He "received the letter from the hand of the messengers and read it; and Hezekiah went up to the house of the LORD and spread it before the LORD. And Hezekiah prayed" (19:14–15).

Hezekiah wasn't going to back down this time. Hezekiah must have been exercising his faith muscles, for at this point he was strong indeed. Listen to his declaration of faith: "Truly, O LORD, the kings of Assyria have laid waste the nations and their lands and have cast their gods into the fire, for they were not gods, but the work of men's hands, wood and stone. Therefore they were destroyed. So now, O LORD our God, save us, please, from his hand, that all the kingdoms of the earth may know that you, O LORD, are God alone" (2 Kings 19:17–19).

And God gladly obliged. That very night the angel of the Lord killed 185,000 men who were encamped around the city. Sennacherib packed his bags and headed back home to his capital city of Nineveh, suddenly deciding maybe he didn't care so much about the little kingdom of Judah.

Just for good measure, God arranged for Sennacherib to meet his end, ironically, as he prayed to his god Nisroch.

When it comes to the little person plus God, it's always a winning combination.

*Read all about Hezekiah's taking on Sennacherib in 2 Kings 18–19, and the parallel story in 2 Chronicles 32 and Isaiah 36–37.*

# A Taxing Situation

*Zacchaeus, a Tax Collector, Finds All He Needs in Jesus*

Factoids: Zacchaeus
- *Domicile:* Jericho
- *Date:* Sometime during Jesus's ministry, around A.D. 30–33
- *Occupation:* Chief tax collector
- *Family Ties:* None mentioned
- *Mentioned in the Bible:* Luke 19:1–10

ZACCHAEUS PEERED DOWN from the branch on which he was half sitting, half lying. The wide canopy of the sycamore tree allowed him to see below without lots of leaves or smaller branches to obstruct his view. He could see the colorful, dusty crowd approaching, following an itinerant preacher named Jesus, a man who apparently said and did amazing things.

Zacchaeus was curious, just like all of the other onlookers who crowded the road outside of Jericho that day. Everyone was talking about this Jesus, and so Zacchaeus thought he'd go and see this latest media darling. If it were happening today, all of the major news networks would have their vans with satellite dishes on top parked beside the city wall. Roving reporters would be sticking their microphones into people's faces, asking them what they knew about Jesus, why they were waiting, what they expected to see. Some enterprising reporter might even climb onto a nearby rock and interview the man in the tree.

Zacchaeus might not have wanted such attention. You see, he wasn't a very popular guy in Jericho. In fact, he was what you might call "despised." His problem? He was a Jewish man who collected taxes from his fellow Jews for the Roman government.

As an occupied nation, the Jews were required to pay taxes to Rome. The Jews hated this heavy burden, knowing that their money went back to finance the occupying army, the temples of pagan gods, and the lascivious lifestyles of Roman leaders. But taxes had to be paid and someone had to collect them. The Romans allowed tax collectors to tack on extra charges over and above the required taxes and keep that money. Hence, tax collectors were also made rich on the backs of their fellow Jews. No wonder they were despised and labeled as traitors.

Zacchaeus was indeed wealthy. He also was very short. That morning, as he arrived with the crowd, he knew he wouldn't be able to see over the shoulders of the taller folks surrounding him. And that's when he thought of the tree. He looked ahead down the main drag where Jesus would be heading and spotted the big sycamore.

He pulled his robe up around his ankles and dashed ahead of the crowd, down the road, and up onto a low-hanging branch, where he spread out to balance himself, and waited.

So here he was, peering down from his perch, watching the advance of the dusty cloud stirred up by the oncoming crowd. It was easy to spot Jesus. He walked at the front of the crowd, talking with those around him yet carrying himself with an unmistakable air of authority. Zacchaeus watched, suddenly beginning to understand what the fuss was all about. This obviously was a very special man.

As Jesus entered the shade of the sycamore tree, he looked up and straight into the eyes of the wealthy man hanging onto the branch—looked at him as if he had already known he was there.

"Zacchaeus, come down immediately. I must stay at your house today" (Luke 19:5 NIV).

*How does this guy know my name?* Zacchaeus must have thought. The authority of the man's bearing and his words required instant compliance. Zacchaeus made his way down the tree, dusted himself off, smiled widely, and led Jesus to his home. As they walked away, the crowd was muttering: "Of all people, why *him*? He's the worst guy ever. Why is Jesus going to *his* house?"

Whatever conversation occurred between the two men on the way and, later, at the meal, we don't know. But something occurred in the tax collector's heart during those few hours as Jesus talked with him. After his encounter with Jesus, Zacchaeus was a changed man: "Zacchaeus stood up and said to the Lord, 'Look, Lord! Here and now I give half of my possessions to the poor, and if I have cheated anybody out of anything, I will pay back four times the amount" (19:8).

Beyond that, Zacchaeus found salvation in Jesus Christ, for Jesus concluded, "Today salvation has come to this house, because this man, too, is a son of Abraham. For the Son of Man came to seek and to save what was lost" (19:9–10).

Even when those he seeks are up in a tree!

*Read the high points of Zacchaeus's close encounter with Jesus in Luke 19:1–10.*

# Nick at Night

*Nicodemus, a Religious Leader, Comes to Jesus at Night*

Factoids: Nicodemus
- *Domicile:* Jerusalem
- *Date:* Around A.D. 30
- *Occupation:* Pharisee; member of the Jewish council
- *Family Ties:* None mentioned, but his contemporaries included Jesus, Caiaphas, Pontius Pilate, and Joseph of Arimathea
- *Mentioned in the Bible:* John 3:1–21, 7:50–52, and 19:38–40

WHAT WAS this prominent Jewish leader doing sneaking around at night? Was he involved in some covert operation or clandestine activity? No, Nicodemus was out late because he was seeking the truth.

A learned teacher himself, Nicodemus came secretly to check out Jesus. He came with questions and he wanted to be taught by Jesus. Nicodemus knew the Old Testament thoroughly and he recognized that the Messianic prophecies were coming true before his eyes. He said to Jesus, "Rabbi, we know you are a teacher who has come from God. For no one could perform the miraculous signs you are doing if God were not with him" (John 3:2 NIV). As he spoke with Jesus that night, he probably got a lot more than he bargained for—including knowledge of salvation and a challenge to lead a new life as a follower of Christ.

As a Pharisee, Nicodemus had his reasons for meeting with Jesus under cover of darkness. Up to this point, and continuing until his death, Jesus' meetings with the Pharisees tended to be confrontational and antagonistic. And that was in broad daylight. Most Pharisees were insanely jealous of Jesus' popularity among the people, and they weren't too crazy about how he challenged their authority and the status quo, and even called them names.

It may have taken a while for him to come out of the dark, but Nicodemus began to display his faith in Jesus by defending him in front of the religious council. As the group discussed possible ways to eliminate Jesus, Nicodemus confronted the Pharisees with their failure to keep their own laws, saying, "Does our law condemn anyone without first hearing him to find out what he is doing?" (John 7:51). It seems he had begun to change and was no longer afraid of what others thought.

The last time Nicodemus is mentioned we find him assisting Joseph of Arimathea with burial preparations for Jesus. There would be no question now of his devotion to the Savior. In this simple act of wrapping Jesus' body for burial with linen, myrrh, and aloes, Nicodemus risked his career and even his life. This was a bold move!

Imagine Nicodemus as he sat in the Jewish council just a few days later: the cacophony of voices, the chaos, and the disbelief when news of Jesus' resurrection reached the Pharisees. As the rest of the group reacted with outrage at the stunning news, Nicodemus probably sat back and allowed a smile to slowly grow upon his face. He might have replayed his life-changing conversation with Jesus in his mind. In his heart, he was praising God for sending the Savior, and deeply humbled that he had had the privilege of learning from the Master in the dark of the night.

*To read the story of Nicodemus, go to John 3:1–21, 7:50, and 19:39.*

# We Three Kings— and Paul

*Paul Pleads His Case Before Felix, Festus, and Agrippa*

PAUL WAS NOT having a very good day. Or a very good year. Actually, make that a couple of years.

Having returned to Jerusalem after completing three missionary journeys, Paul walked into a hornet's nest of trouble. He was arrested, was brought before the Jewish ruling council, was slapped around, endured a plot against his life, and finally was taken to the prison in Caesarea—accompanied by a detachment of two hundred soldiers, seventy horsemen, and two hundred spearmen (Acts 23:23).

Overkill? Well, Paul had been known to slip out of prisons and have earthquakes set him free. If word had gotten around about this slippery prisoner, such precautions were not unreasonable.

Hence Paul arrived on the doorstep of Felix, Roman governor of the province of Judea. (Incidentally, this was the same position that Pontius Pilate had held.) When his Jewish accusers arrived from Jerusalem, Felix heard the case against Paul. But in the end, Felix put Paul back in prison and kept him there, hoping that Paul would come up with some bribe money for his freedom.

Two years went by. Felix lost his job and was called back to Rome, and a new governor arrived in Caesarea. Festus wasted no time in dealing with Paul's languishing case and resumed his trial. Once again Paul's accusers were summoned to Caesarea, and the whole thing started over again.

But this time Paul was getting tired of sitting in prison; he wanted to be out sharing the gospel message. Two years had gone by. In an effort to move things ahead, he made a bold move:

> "I am now standing before Caesar's court, where I ought to be tried. I have not done any wrong to the Jews, as you yourself know very well. If, however, I am guilty of doing anything deserving death, I do not refuse to die. But if the charges brought against me by these Jews are not true, no one has the right to hand me over to them. I appeal to Caesar!" After Festus had conferred with his council, he declared: "You have appealed to Caesar. To Caesar you will go!" (Acts 25:10–12 NIV)

As a citizen of Rome, Paul was within his rights to appeal to the emperor. It didn't mean that Caesar himself would necessarily hear his case, but that a higher court would hear it—sort of like taking something to the Supreme Court.

Enter king number three, Agrippa, ruler over northern and eastern Palestine. He and his wife came to visit Festus, and Paul's case came up in their discussion. Paul came out once again to tell his story and, of course, he shared the gospel message.

But, like the other two kings before him, Agrippa just didn't get it. "Agrippa said to Paul, 'Do you think that in such a short time you can persuade me to be a Christian?'" (Acts 26:28).

And the prisoner in chains responded to the king and everyone else in the throne room that day: "Short time or long—I pray God that not only you but all who are listening to me today may become what I am, except for these chains" (26:29).

Paul may have been having a rough couple of years, but he knew that wherever he was, God's hand was on him.

*For the story of Paul's conversations with these three kings, read Acts 24–26.*

# Divisive Diotrephes

## Diotrephes's Pride Causes Problems

THERE'S AN OLD Abbott and Costello routine involving baseball, a number of misunderstandings, and the immortal line "Who's on first?" Diotrephes, a first-century church member, had his own routine about who was on first—he was. But the apostle John wasn't laughing.

As part of his apostolic ministry, John wrote letters to the church congregations under his supervision. He provided two attaboys—one to Gaius, to whom the letter was addressed, and one to Demetrius—for their good works and faithfulness as God's children. They obviously took John's advice about loving others—"Dear friends, let us love one another, for love comes from God" (1 John 4:7 NIV)—to heart.

Sandwiched between these commendations was a huge criticism concerning the negative behavior of Diotrephes, one of the leaders in the congregation. Diotrephes refused to provide hospitality to the missionaries who visited his church and city. Not only that, he told his congregation not to host any missionaries. If anyone in his congregation hosted a missionary, Diotrephes kicked the host out of the church.

John did not provide reasons for Diotrephes's consistently inhospitable behavior, other than his need to "be first." Being hospitable wasn't just the proper thing to do; it was the custom of that day to provide housing for strangers and temporary residents, especially since inns were few and far between and were at times extremely dangerous to stay in. Traveling missionaries depended on the support of other believers. This is why John and other epistle writers urged believers to extend hospitality. For example: "Don't forget to show hospitality to strangers, for some who have done this have entertained angels without realizing it!" (Hebrews 13:2 NLT). "Offer hospitality to one another without grumbling" (1 Peter 4:9 NIV). "When God's people are in need, be ready to help them. Always be eager to practice hospitality" (Romans 12:13 NLT).

Diotrephes's behavior was in direct opposition to his duty and was an abuse of authority. Having written a previous letter that undoubtedly was ignored by Diotrephes, John bluntly stated, "Don't let this bad example influence you. Follow only what is good. Remember that those who do good prove that they are God's children, and those who do evil prove that they do not know God" (3 John 11).

Perhaps Diotrephes should have remembered the words of Jesus: "But many who are now first will be last" (Matthew 19:30 CEV).

*To read the story of Diotrephes, see 3 John 9–11.*

### Proud People and What Became of Them

"Those who walk in pride [God] is able to humble" (Daniel 4:37 ESV). Truer words were never spoken. And the man who spoke them—Nebuchadnezzar—learned that the hard way, along with many others in the Bible.

| Proud Person/People | How He or She Was Humbled |
| --- | --- |
| Hagar | Hagar, the concubine of Abram, grew proud when she could conceive a child (Ishmael) and Sarah could not. After Sarah mistreated her, Hagar ran away into the desert. But an angel told her to return and submit to Sarah (Genesis 16). |
| Pharaoh | Pharaoh tried to hold on to his pride by holding on to the enslaved people of Israel. But after ten plagues, he finally agreed to let them go—only to renege. At the Red Sea, Pharaoh and his army met a watery end (Exodus 5–14). |
| Miriam | Feeling envious of Moses, Miriam egged on her brother Aaron to help her speak against Moses because of his marriage. But God punished Miriam by striking her with leprosy (Numbers 12). |
| Goliath of Gath | This gigantic champion of the Philistines was cut down to size by the much smaller David, who came against him in the name of the Lord for taunting the army of God's people (1 Samuel 17). |
| Rehoboam | After rejecting the advice of the elder advisers of his father in favor of the younger men, Rehoboam threatened to treat the people of Israel badly. And they rebelled. When Rehoboam tried to take Judah to war against Israel, God told him not to go. The kingdom of Israel split into northern and southern kingdoms (1 Kings 12:1–24). |

| PROUD PERSON/PEOPLE | HOW HE OR SHE WAS HUMBLED |
|---|---|
| Gehazi | Feeling that he was owed something by Naaman, the Syrian healed of leprosy, Gehazi lied to Naaman in the hopes of gaining the reward that Elisha spurned. But when Elisha found out about Gehazi's deception, Gehazi was struck with leprosy (2 Kings 5:20–27). |
| Jezebel | Long before Jezebel died, Elijah prophesied what would become of the proud queen (see 1 Kings 21:23). When King Jehu of Israel went to Jezreel, he spotted her at a window and commanded that she be thrown down. As Elijah predicted, her remains were left for the dogs (2 Kings 9:30–37). |
| Athaliah | When proud Athaliah usurped the throne to become queen by killing the members of the royal family, Joash was hidden by his nurse. Jehoiada, the priest, ordered her to be put to death (2 Kings 11:1–16). |
| Sennacherib | The proud Assyrian king taunted King Hezekiah of Judah. After Hezekiah prayed, God promised to deliver Israel. He sent one angel, who killed 185,000 Assyrian soldiers. Sennacherib hastily withdrew and was assassinated upon his return home (2 Kings 18–19). |
| Uzziah, the king of Judah | Although obedient to the Lord, Uzziah allowed his success as king to go to his head. When he tried to burn incense to the Lord after the priests warned him not to, he was struck with leprosy (2 Chronicles 26). |

| Proud Person/People | How He or She Was Humbled |
|---|---|
| Hezekiah | Good King Hezekiah was not above pride. When he reacted in pride after being healed of an illness, God grew angry. But Hezekiah repented (2 Chronicles 32:24–26). Following that event, when envoys came from Babylon, Hezekiah proudly showed them all of his riches, and Isaiah condemned Hezekiah for doing so (32:31; see also 2 Kings 20:12–19). |
| The people of Israel | Like many other prophets, Isaiah prophesied against the pride of Israel. God would allow enemy nations to defeat Israel (Isaiah 9:8–21). |
| The king of Assyria | Although God allowed the Assyrians to capture many of the Israelites, Isaiah prophesied that the Lord would deal with the pride of the king of Assyria (Isaiah 10:12–13). |
| Moab | Through the prophet Isaiah, God promised that Moab's pride would be shattered within three years (Isaiah 15–16). |
| Babylon | Jeremiah prophesied against Babylon—the proud nation that carried off many of Israel's people. God planned to stir up other nations against them (Jeremiah 50). |
| Egypt | Ezekiel spoke against the "proud strength" of Egypt. Ezekiel predicted that Egypt's allies would fail and Egypt would "fall by the sword" (Ezekiel 30:6 NIV). |
| Nebuchadnezzar | The proud king of Babylon gave himself a pat on the back as he surveyed his wonderful palace. But when God allowed him to suffer a bout of insanity, Nebuchadnezzar realized that the true king of the world was God (Daniel 4). |

| PROUD PERSON/PEOPLE | HOW HE OR SHE WAS HUMBLED |
|---|---|
| Belshazzar | Belshazzar, who didn't learn from Nebuchadnezzar's example, was killed right after Daniel interpreted the message written on a wall (Daniel 5). |
| Edom | Through the prophet Obadiah, God had harsh words for the proud nation of Edom: "See I will make you small among the nations; you will be utterly despised" (Obadiah 2 NIV). |
| Pharisees, Sadducees, and other teachers of the law | Jesus pronounced seven "woes" against the proud, hypocritical leaders of Israel. The blood of martyred people from Abel to Zechariah would be on their hands (Matthew 23:1–36). |
| A Pharisee | Jesus told a parable of a Pharisee and a tax collector. While the Pharisee congratulated himself for his deeds, the tax collector sought God's mercy. Jesus explained that the tax collector, rather than the Pharisee, would receive God's forgiveness (Luke 18:9–14). |
| Herod Agrippa I | Herod gave a speech that was so eloquent that the people proclaimed him to be a god—to which he apparently agreed. He was killed by the angel of the Lord and eaten by worms (Acts 12:20–22). |
| Satan | John prophesied the downfall of the dragon—Satan—who after being bound for one thousand years and defeated by the army of heaven, will wind up in the lake of fire (Revelation 20:1–10). |

# PART THREE

# Leaders and Laborers

# An Ark in the Park

*Noah Builds an Ark on Dry Land*

Factoids: Noah
- *Domicile:* We aren't told how far from the Garden of Eden people began to settle
- *Date:* Undated (earlier than 3000 B.C.)
- *Occupation:* Farmer, shipbuilder, preacher
- *Family Ties:* Grandfather, Methuselah; father, Lamech; sons, Shem, Ham, and Japheth
- *Mentioned in the Bible:* Genesis 5:29–10:32; 1 Chronicles 1:3; Isaiah 54:9; Ezekiel 14:14, 20; Matthew 24:37–38; Luke 3:36; 17:26–27; Hebrews 11:7; 1 Peter 3:20; 2 Peter 2:5

NOAH HAD HIS WORK cut out for him. He took a deep breath as he fumbled around looking for another long piece of cypress to measure and cut: "Measure twice, cut once." He saw two of his neighbors walk by and couldn't help overhearing their conversation.

Man 1: "Hey, what's that guy building?"
Man 2: "I don't know, but it sure is going to be big!"
Man 3: "I heard he's building a boat."
Man 1 and 2: "A boat?" (uproarious laughter)

Noah wiped his brow and felt very tired. *Couldn't they let up a little?* he wondered.

When God gave the instructions for building this great boat, he told Noah: "Make yourself an ark of cypress wood; make rooms in it and coat it with pitch inside and out. This is how you are to build it: The ark is to be 450 feet long, 75 feet wide and 45 feet high. Make a roof for it and finish the ark to within 18 inches of the top. Put a door in the side of the ark and make lower, middle and upper decks" (Genesis 6:14–16 NIV).

Imagine building a boat the length of one and a half football fields and as tall as a four-story building! What probably caused this to be even more of a spectacle—and even more ridiculous in the minds of the onlookers—was that this boat was built on dry land. Yep, an ark in the park.

So why did God tell Noah to build an ark? The human race had become extremely violent and God was able to find only one righteous man: Noah. After only a few generations, the number of people who knew and worshipped the God of Creation had dwindled to one small family. "Noah was a righteous man, blameless among the people of his time, and he walked with God" (6:9). God told Noah that he would destroy all life on earth with the exception of Noah and his family.

When people stopped and asked Noah why he was building an ark so far from water, surely he told them what God had said. But they didn't get it. God was actually giving them a chance to repent through Noah's very visual testimony of coming destruction. And a long chance it was—in all likelihood Noah spent around 120 years building the ark. For more than a century Noah worked and warned—and all he got for his trouble was scorn and ridicule.

For Noah, obedience to God meant a serious commitment to a long-term project. In our fast-paced twenty-first-century society we often have trouble sticking to a project for a few hours. But Noah was committed to seeing it through, though it would take almost two of today's human lifespans.

When it was finished, Noah and his family were spared from the deadly flood of water that followed the "flood" of sinful wickedness, both of which proved to be destructive to mankind. Noah's dedication and obedience showed that God is faithful to those who follow him.

*To read all about Noah's shipbuilding experience, read Genesis 6:9–22.*

# Tower of Trouble

## Some People Try to Build a Tower to Heaven

PEOPLE OF ANCIENT TIMES might seem a bit silly to us today. Because science has allowed us to know where our atmosphere ends and where space begins, we can scoff at the idea of a group of people believing they'd build a tower that would reach heaven. What were they thinking?

This tower was most likely a ziggurat, a pyramid-shaped structure with ramps or steps going up the sides. A lot of ancient cities built these types of structures, which were used primarily as temples. They normally stood around three hundred feet high, a far cry from reaching the heavens. So what was so important about this particular tower that God "came down to see the city and the tower that the men were building" (Genesis 11:5 NIV)?

Scripture tells us that "the whole world had one language and a common speech" (11:1), so no matter where people lived, they could communicate with one another. A particular group of people settled in the plain of Shinar (between the Tigris and Euphrates rivers in present-day Iraq) and set about the task of establishing a city. But the people of the earth, once again, had forgotten about God. They began to see themselves as very important and wanted to build a monument to themselves and their achievements.

"They said to each other, 'Come, let's make bricks and bake them thoroughly. . . . Come, let us build ourselves a city, with a tower that reaches to the heavens, so that we may make a name for ourselves and not be scattered over the face of the whole earth'" (11:3–4). These people believed that this tower would be the focal point of their city, a monument to their greatness for all the world to marvel at for generations to come.

The Lord put a swift end to their self-promotion. He saw the tower they were building, but moreover, he saw the intent of their hearts. By confusing their language, God reduced this large mass of people into many small tribes. Suddenly, the most important thing in life wasn't world fame but finding someone who spoke the same language.

The monuments we build for ourselves today might consist of important job titles, fancy cars, expensive homes, and designer clothes—all to draw attention to our achievements and successes. While possessing these things isn't necessarily wrong, when we allow them to possess *us* they take God's rightful place in our lives. Have you built any towers in your life that take the place of God?

*To read about the Tower of Babel, see Genesis 11:1–9.*

# Say Uncle!

*Abram (Abraham) Amasses an Army to Pursue His Captured Nephew Lot*

Factoids: Abram (later Abraham)
- *Domicile:* Hebron, near the great trees of Mamre in Canaan
- *Date:* Sometime after 2091 B.C.
- *Occupation:* Wealthy landowner and herdsman
- *Family Ties:* Wife, Sarai (later named Sarah); father, Terah; brothers, Nahor and Haran; nephew, Lot; sister-in-law, Milcah; sons, Ishmael and Isaac
- *Mentioned in the Bible:* Genesis 11:26–25:11; 26:1–5, 18, 24; 28:4, 9, 13; 31:42, 53; 32:9; 48:15–16; 49:29–31; 50:13, 24; Exodus 2:24; 3:6, 16; 4:5; 6:3; 32:13; 33:1; Leviticus 26:42; Matthew 1:1–2; Luke 1:55; 3:34; John 8:58; Acts 7:2–8; Romans 4; Galatians 36–16; Hebrews 2:16; 6:13–14, 7:1–9; 11:8–12

Factoids: Lot
- *Domicile:* Sodom
- *Date:* Sometime after 2091 B.C.
- *Occupation:* City official, wealthy landowner, and herdsman
- *Family Ties:* Wife, unnamed; two daughters, unnamed; uncle, Abram; father, Haran; grandsons, Moab and Ben-Ammi

- *Mentioned in the Bible:* Genesis 11:27, 31; 12:4; 13:1–14; 14:1, 12–16; 19:1–38; Deuteronomy 2:9; Luke 17:28–29, 32; 2 Peter 2:7–8

M OST OF US probably could not imagine an elderly man gathering an army and riding off to rescue a family member. Such a scenario sounds too weird to believe. Yet that's exactly the scenario Abram, the elderly man, was facing. It all began with lots of kings, a couple of wars, and the victor's spoils.

When God told Abram to move to Canaan, Abram's nephew Lot went with him. They both were quite wealthy, with much livestock, flocks, and herds—and lots of people to take care of it all. It's not surprising that arguing ensued between their hired hands. After a while, Abram suggested that they separate to keep the peace. Lot chose to move to the well-watered region of Sodom, while Abram moved to Hebron (see Genesis 13).

Sadly, war swiftly became the norm in the region. Four kings, two of whom were Amraphel (the king of Shinar) and Kedorlaomer (the king of Elam), defeated the armies of five kings (over Sodom, Gomorrah, Admah, Zeboiim, and Bela). But after being ruled by Kedorlaomer for twelve years, the five defeated kings decided to fight against their oppressors.

A second defeat occurred, which resulted in the seizing of the possessions and people of the kings of Sodom and Gomorrah. Lot was included in the tally of captured people.

Enter the hero—Abram. Now, Abram was no longer a young man. He was seventy-five way back when God first called him to leave his homeland (Genesis 12:4). Although we don't know his exact age here, he was obviously older, though not yet ready for retirement or AARP coupons.

Abram was at home when one man who had escaped ran in, out of breath. He told his master about the battle and his nephew's capture. The fact that the person reported to Abram says a lot about Abram's reputation.

Quickly marshaling his "posse"—a fighting force of 318 skilled men—Abram headed off in pursuit. After splitting the troops, Abram and his men attacked and were victorious. Their being able to do what the armies of five kings could not do hints at God's hand in Abram's life. The descriptive action of the final verse in this story shows the hero Abram finishing the job and riding off into the sunset: "He brought back all the possessions, and also brought back his kinsman Lot with his possessions, and the women and the people" (Genesis 14:16 ESV).

*To read all about Abram's daring rescue of Lot, see Genesis 14:1–16.*

# Death on the Nile

*Midwives Labor Against a Bad Leader—and Save the Hebrew Boys*

RUTHLESS. That's the only way to describe a leader who decides that the best way to handle a difficult situation is to kill all baby boys as soon as they're born. And courageous is the only way to describe the two women laborers who defied the leader's orders.

The Hebrew people had been in Egypt for a long time. They arrived there as a company of seventy people when the Hebrew man Joseph was second-in-command in Egypt. (Read the story in Genesis 46.) Time passed and that little company of seventy "multiplied and grew exceedingly strong, so that the land was filled with them" (Exodus 1:7 ESV).

Well, along comes a new pharaoh. He didn't know anything about Joseph. (Perhaps he fell asleep in Egyptian history class and didn't hear how Joseph had done a few little things like saved his nation from starvation.) As the new pharaoh looked around at all these Hebrew folks, he got worried. He thought that if some other nation came along and attacked Egypt, the Hebrews might join the enemy and make a force even his army couldn't withstand. So he decided to put all the Hebrew people into slavery.

Yeah. Good idea. Great way to win the people's loyalty, Pharaoh.

Problem was, the Hebrew people just kept multiplying. Seems like the hard work and harsh labor didn't stop babies from being born.

Then Pharaoh had a really awful idea. He had a private audience with two Hebrew midwives. These women must have had their beepers going off constantly as they helped the fruitful Hebrew women give birth! Pharaoh commanded Shiphrah and Puah to kill any baby boy who was born, but they could let the baby girls live (how thoughtful). Apparently, they were to make it seem that the baby boys were just born dead. Pharaoh hoped, in this way, to surreptitiously lower the number of Hebrew men who might grow up and join the imaginary army that was amassing against him.

The text doesn't tell us if Pharaoh threatened the midwives with death for disobedience because they were slaves, or if he bribed them with better conditions or even freedom for their obedience. All we know about these two women is this: "The midwives feared God and did not do as the king of Egypt commanded them, but let the male children live" (1:17).

Pharaoh was not pleased. He saw that babies were not being killed, so he called the two women before him again. "What's going on?" he asked.

And they did what any fearful slave who has disobeyed the ultimate leader would do.

They lied.

Basically they said that the Egyptian women were weak, but the Hebrew women (no doubt because of the hard work inflicted on them as slaves) were strong and could have their babies before the midwives got there. At that point it was too late to kill the babies.

Pharaoh was getting desperate. The surreptitious route wasn't working; better be more direct. "Then Pharaoh commanded all his people, 'Every son that is born to the Hebrews you shall cast into the Nile, but you shall let every daughter live'" (1:22).

Whether Pharaoh sent soldiers out or offered rewards to his citizens for tossing babies into the river is uncertain from the text. The reign of terror surely was horrific to the Hebrew families—and especially to the pregnant women.

One family had an interesting way of dealing with the issue. They put their baby boy in the Nile just as Pharaoh commanded—but in a nice little floating basket. And that's how Moses survived the baby holocaust and grew up to set his nation free.

Sometimes desperate times call for desperate measures.

*The ruthless pharaoh's command about the babies is recorded in Exodus 1.*

# The Burden of Bricks

## The Hebrew People Slave Away in Egypt

THE ATHEIST GERMAN PHILOSOPHER Friedrich Nietzsche once said, "What does not destroy me makes me stronger." Tell that to the Hebrew slaves in ancient Egypt. Suffering under horrible conditions, they may have gotten stronger physically, but they also were slowly being burdened to exhaustion.

Four hundred years had passed since Joseph had moved his family to Goshen, the land just north of Pharaoh's great cities (Genesis 47:1–12). In that span, the Egyptians forgot about Joseph, the great Hebrew dream interpreter, and how he saved Egypt from starvation. Furthermore, the Hebrew nation had grown from one small tribe to two million strong. To Egypt's new pharaoh, the nation of Israel was a huge threat. What if they decided to wage war or sided with an enemy of Egypt? How could he keep them under his control?

His answer was to enslave them.

There were degrees of slavery in Egypt. Some slaves worked all day in the blazing sun, cutting stone or baking bricks. Others were skilled artisans such as jewelers, seamstresses, and carpenters. Nevertheless, a slave was a slave was a slave—all were treated ruthlessly. Pharaoh tried to break the spirit of the Hebrew people, but instead they multiplied and grew stronger. And what's more, they cried out to God in their distress, and God came to the rescue through a man named Moses (see Exodus 2:23–3:10).

Moses's first attempts to reason with Pharaoh went nowhere.

God had told Moses to expect this, saying that Pharaoh's heart would be hardened. When Moses demanded that Pharaoh free the Hebrew people in order to go worship the Lord, Pharaoh scoffed, "Who is this Lord? I don't know anything about him, and there's no way I'm letting Israel go." Then he ordered the slave drivers and foremen: "You are no longer to supply the people with straw for making bricks; let them go and gather their own straw. But require them to make the same number of bricks as before; don't reduce the quota. They are lazy; that is why they are crying out, 'Let us go and sacrifice to our God.' Make the work harder for the men so that they keep working and pay no attention to lies" (5:7–9 NIV).

Ouch. Not good if you were in the slave brick brigade. Caught in the middle of the power struggle, the slaves turned on Moses. In their distress they didn't see the big picture. But ten miraculous plagues and a divided Red Sea later, as they headed out of Egypt a free people, they began to understand.

*To read the whole story of how the Israelites labored under the Egyptians, see Exodus 1–6.*

# The Gift
# That Keeps on Giving

*Bezalel and Oholiab Use Their Gifts*

GOD WANTED the Hebrews to do things properly, especially when it came to worship.

The Israelites had been languishing in slavery in Egypt for so long that they did not have a way to worship, much less a place of their own in which to worship . . . until now. When God delivered them and they were leaving Egypt (after Pharaoh finally let them go), they plundered their captors' riches on their way out of town (Exodus 12:35–36). What was the purpose of taking all that gold, silver, bronze, rich fabric, and precious gems? God had a plan.

God told Moses, detail by detail, how every inch of the tabernacle was to be made and furnished. There was a use for everything, from the ark of the covenant to the curtains, from the lampstands to the linen robes of the priests. After writing out scrolls and scrolls of instructions, Moses must have been thinking, *Great. I know what I'm supposed to do. Now who am I going to get to do it?* "Then the LORD said to Moses, 'See, I have chosen Bezalel son of Uri, the son of Hur, of the tribe of Judah, and I have filled him with the Spirit of God, with skill, ability and knowledge in all kinds of crafts—to make artistic designs for work in gold, silver and bronze, to cut and set stones, to work in wood, and to engage in all kinds of craftsmanship' (31:1–5 NIV).

Okay, so there's one really talented guy. But could he do it all? Surely he would need some help.

God continued, "Moreover, I have appointed Oholiab son of Ahisamach, of the tribe of Dan, to help him. Also I have given skill to all the craftsmen to make everything I have commanded you" (31:6).

When we undertake a task, such as remodeling a room or refurbishing an old vehicle, we might go online for some information or buy a book for helpful advice. When we build something brand-new, we (most of us, anyway) read the instructions. After all, it would be unthinkable to try to assemble a bicycle without reading the manual! Bezalel and Oholiab didn't have the benefit of hundreds of online experts or books written by the pros. But they had something far better: God's instructions and God's gifting for the task.

These two men—and all the craftsmen under them—were blessed with the gift of craftsmanship. They were told what to make out of gold, where to use the precious stones, and the dimensions of things. Other than that, the artistic designs were up to them. Imagine the fun these guys had decorating the very first tabernacle for their God!

Don't ever be fooled into thinking that some of the abilities God gives people are less important than others. Without the abilities of Bezalel and Oholiab, Moses and the Hebrews would not have had a beautiful place to worship God.

*Read about these gifted men in Exodus 31:1–11.*

# Only the Lonely

*Caleb and Joshua Stand Alone Against the Crowd*

Factoids: Caleb

- *Domicile:* Egypt, to the wilderness, to the Promised Land
- *Date:* About 1400 B.C.
- *Occupation:* Soldier, shepherd, spy
- *Family Ties:* Father, Jephunneh; brother, Kenaz; daughter, Acsah
- *Mentioned in the Bible:* Numbers 13–14; Joshua 14–15; Judges 1:12–20; 1 Chronicles 4:15

SOMETIMES BEING a good leader means being able to stand up for what's right. Even if you have to stand alone.

Just ask Caleb.

God had freed the Hebrew nation from slavery in Egypt (see "The Prophet and the Pharaoh," page 119). When God first brought this proposition to Moses, he said, "I have come down to rescue [my people] from the hand of the Egyptians and to bring them up out of that land into a good and spacious land, a land flowing with milk and honey—the home of the Canaanites, Hittites, Amorites, Perizzites, Hivites and Jebusites" (Exodus 3:8 NIV). That "land" became known as the Promised Land. After a stop at Mount Sinai to receive the Ten Commandments and other laws that would guide this new young nation, Moses led the people north toward the land that would be theirs.

Only it didn't all work out so well. Upon arriving in the Desert of Paran, south of what would eventually become Israel, the Lord told Moses to send out spies (read about that mission in "Learning the Hard Way," page 7). When they returned, everyone came to hear the report. The spies showed the fruit of the land, but also reported that the cities were large and fortified, the people were powerful, and there were descendants of Anak (meaning large people, giants).

So Caleb piped up, "Alrighty then. Good report. Let's go take the land!"

One can almost see him dashing back to his tent, grabbing his military gear, jogging past the group, and suddenly stopping to realize that no one was following him. The other spies turned back to the crowd and stated their conclusion: "We can't take the land."

Wait a minute! God was *giving* them the land! In fact, as the entire nation began to grumble about having left Egypt in the first place, only two spies, Caleb and Joshua, stood strong. "If the LORD is pleased with us, he will lead us into that land, a land flowing with milk and honey, and will give it to us" (Numbers 14:8). "C'mon, guys! It's gonna be fine!" they urged.

But it wasn't fine. In fact, it was a nightmare. The people talked about stoning Caleb and Joshua.

Then the Lord got involved. Basically, his response to the people's faithlessness was this: "Okay, you wanna be afraid? Fine. Then don't go into the land. In fact, I'm not going to *let* you go in. Instead, you get to wander around in the desert for forty years until every last one of you scaredy-cats is dead (except for Caleb and Joshua). Then, I'll let your children go in and take possession of this bountiful land I've promised."

So the nation turned back around and began a long trek to nowhere in the desert. Even Caleb and Joshua had to turn around and follow along. Some reward for faithfulness—imagine how ticked they must have been! In the end, however, it was fine for them. Joshua got to lead the people into the land, and as he parceled out the land, the Lord gave Caleb a special portion—his own city. Read about that in Joshua 14:6–15.

Caleb remained faithful to God, and God was faithful to him. Sometimes only the lonely are truly with God.

*The story of Caleb and Joshua's courageous stand is told in Numbers 13–14.*

# Just Do It

## Joshua Steps into Really Big Shoes

Factoids: Joshua

- *Domicile:* Egypt; Desert of Sinai; Canaan (the Promised Land)
- *Date:* About 1400 B.C.
- *Occupation:* Special assistant to Moses; warrior; leader
- *Family Ties:* Father, Nun
- *Mentioned in the Bible:* Exodus 17:9–14; 24:13; 32:17; 33:11; Numbers 11:28; 13:16; 14:6–10; 26:65; 27:18–23; 32:11–12, 28; 34:17; Deuteronomy 1:38; 3:21, 28; 31:3, 7, 14, 23; 34:9; the book of Joshua; Judges 2:6–9; 1 Kings 16:34

A NYONE WHO HAS EVER tried to fill the shoes of a great leader knows that people can't help but make comparisons. "She never did it that way!" or "I can't believe he's not following tradition!" are only a few comments that undermine the new leader's authority. Yet succession is a reality. And one of the best tests of leadership is the willingness and ability to train a successor. Some leaders, paranoid that someone younger will edge them out of their job, refuse to share their wisdom. When that happens, the successor—and the job he or she inherits—often fails.

Moses was a great leader—ever since the day he first marched hesitantly into the mighty Pharaoh's courtroom and demanded that he free an entire nation of slaves. But Moses was getting old, and God told him that he would not lead the nation into the Promised Land. In fact, God had already chosen Moses's successor: "Take Joshua son of Nun, a man in whom is the spirit, and lay your hand on him. . . . Give him some of your authority so the whole Israelite community will obey him" (Numbers 27:18, 20 NIV).

So who, exactly, was Joshua?

When the Hebrew people first left Egypt, they were given the opportunity to go directly to the Promised Land (Canaan). This was the land God promised to them—hence the name "Promised Land." When they arrived at the border, God told Moses to send twelve spies (one from each tribe) to explore the land and begin the tactical planning the Hebrews would need to conquer it. Joshua was one of the twelve spies (Numbers 13).

Ten of the spies came back from their exploratory jaunt too scared to fight the people who lived in the land. Joshua and Caleb were the only two spies to have complete faith and confidence that God would deliver on his promise and help them conquer the land. But the people wanted to stone them! (See "Only the Lonely," the story just before this one.)

Disappointed in his people's lack of faith, God condemned that generation to wander the desert for forty years, and added that no one who had been in slavery in Egypt, with the exception of Joshua and Caleb, would see the Promised Land.

As Moses's assistant, Joshua had on-the-job training for forty years. He had the privilege of experiencing firsthand what it meant to lead God's people. As the children of the wandering Hebrews grew up, you can be sure they were reminded often by their parents of the importance of faith and obedience to God.

After all of the disobedient generation passed away, it was Moses's turn. God took him to a mountaintop and showed him the Promised Land. Immediately afterward he died, and Joshua took over. Right away God gave Joshua his first orders: "Moses my servant is dead. Now then, you and all these people, get ready to cross the Jordan River into the land I am about to give to them—to the Israelites. I will give you every place where you set your foot, as I promised Moses" (Joshua 1:2–3).

God gave Joshua two strategies for success as he filled the leadership role:

First, God reminded Joshua four times to be strong and courageous (1:6, 7, 9, 18). In other words, "Just do it, Josh." The task at hand would not be easy, but knowing that God was with him would bring strength and courage.

Also, Joshua needed to study and obey the Book of the Law (God's Word). "Do not let this Book of the Law depart from your mouth; meditate on it day and night, so that you may be careful to do everything written in it. Then you will be prosperous and successful" (1:8).

Anyone in leadership knows that strength, courage, and abiding by the rule book are essential for accomplishing goals. Joshua had big shoes to fill, but with God's help, he succeeded.

*To read about Joshua's first steps in big shoes, see Joshua 1:1–9.*

# A Monumental Task

*As They Enter the Promised Land, the Israelites Celebrate with Twelve Stones*

AFTER FORTY LONG YEARS of wilderness wandering, the time had come for God's people to enter the Promised Land. This was a huge undertaking, so how would they know that God was really with them? Well, God had that all worked out. Here's what leader Joshua told them:

> Today you will know that the living God is among you. He will surely drive out the Canaanites, Hittites, Hivites, Perizzites, Girgashites, Amorites, and Jebusites ahead of you. Look, the Ark of the Covenant, which belongs to the LORD of the whole earth, will lead you across the Jordan River! Now choose twelve men from the tribes of Israel, one from each tribe. The priests will carry the Ark of the LORD, the LORD of all the earth. As soon as their feet touch the water, the flow of water will be cut off upstream, and the river will stand up like a wall. (Joshua 3:10–13 NLT)

That sounded a little familiar, didn't it? Perhaps a streak of electric excitement shot through the throngs as they talked amongst themselves. "Just like when our forefathers were delivered from slavery in Egypt! Imagine that!" And it all happened just as God and Joshua said. As soon as the priests carrying the ark stepped into the water, the upstream water stopped miles away, thus cutting off the downstream water. All of the Israelites could now safely cross the Jordan River. The people quickly passed through on dry ground, landing in the Promised Land, high and dry.

But while the priests remained in the middle of the river, God told them that a special monument was to be constructed to remember this event. God explained to Joshua, "Choose twelve men, one from each tribe. Tell them, 'Take twelve stones from the very place where the priests are standing in the middle of the Jordan. Carry them out and pile them up at the place where you will camp tonight'" (4:2–3).

Stones were certainly more permanent than a scrapbook or a souvenir T-shirt inscribed *I survived forty years of wandering in the desert*. So twelve men from each tribe were picked to do the hard labor. Each one chose a large stone from the riverbed and carried it to Israel's camp. Joshua then created a sturdy memorial for generations to remember what God had done for them at that place. And remembering God's strong hand in their return to the land was a great way to begin their new lives on the other side of the Jordan.

Once the memorial was complete, God allowed the priests to come out of the riverbed. The moment they touched land, the Jordan River began flooding its banks as it had prior to the priests' arrival. That day the Israelites knew God was with Joshua, and they respected him as much as they had Moses.

*To learn more about the Israelites' river walk and stone memorial, read Joshua 3–4.*

# Under Construction

*Solomon Drafts Workers to Build Israel's First Temple*

Factoids: Solomon
- *Domicile:* Jerusalem
- *Date:* Around 970 B.C.
- *Occupation:* King of Israel
- *Family Ties:* Father, David; mother, Bathsheba; brothers, Absalom, Adonijah; sister, Tamar; son, Rehoboam
- *Mentioned in the Bible:* 2 Samuel 12:24; 1 Kings 11:43; 1 Chronicles 28–29; 2 Chronicles 1–10; Nehemiah 13:26; Psalm 72; Matthew 6:29; 12:42

WHEN A MODERN BUILDING is being constructed, we are bombarded by the noise of cranes hoisting, pneumatic drills drilling, and hammers hammering. So one can imagine the sounds in ancient times when the first temple in Jerusalem was built. But if the sound of a hammer falling or chisels chiseling is part of the imaginary landscape in our minds, we would be totally wrong. At the temple building site, no such sounds were heard.

When David was king of Israel, he greatly desired to build a temple—an earthly house for God where the people could worship him. And although God said no to David's request through the prophet Nathan, he told David that David's son Solomon would build the temple. (See 2 Samuel 7:5–7 and 1 Chronicles 22.) While David was described as a man of war, Solomon was called "a man of rest" (1 Chronicles 22:9 ESV)—well suited to the task of building the temple.

The awesome and intricate plans David made for the construction of the temple aided Solomon in this task. David collected iron, silver, gold, bronze, precious gems, marble, and cedar logs. He had a list of all the best carpenters and stonemasons on speed dial. He also asked the people to give an offering for the temple project. They were more than willing to give gold and gems.

After David's death, Solomon sent a gracious letter to Hiram, the king of Tyre, telling Hiram of his project and asking him to provide pine and cedar logs, as well as manpower. In exchange, Solomon would give him wheat and olive oil. The arrangement suited Hiram and a treaty followed.

Now came the hard part: building the temple. For that task, thirty thousand Israelite laborers were drafted into the project. This was not voluntary labor. They *had* to serve, just as they would have if drafted into the army. So off they went—ten thousand each month. They worked one month and were allowed to go home for two months.

But this was not the entire workforce. Eighty thousand stonecutters and seventy thousand other laborers from other lands were drafted. These workers were supervised by nearly four thousand foremen.

To make the foundation of the temple, the laborers had to move heavy stone blocks from the quarry to the building site for positioning. Since these stones were cut at the quarry, no hammering or chiseling took place at the building site (1 Kings 6:7).

The temple was modeled after the tabernacle, but on a grander scale. The walls were made of cedar and the floors made of pine. Within the temple a very special place called the most holy place (Sanctum Sanctorum) was constructed. There, the ark of the covenant was kept beneath two carved cherubim covered in gold.

To make the furnishings of the temple—the pillars, a huge basin in which water was kept, the twelve bulls on which the basin sat, bronze lampstands, and many other items—a highly skilled man named Huram from Tyre was drafted. For the other furnishings, gold figured heavily. There was a golden altar, a golden table on which the showbread (the bread of the Presence) was kept, gold basins, gold lampstands, and much more.

All of the work on the temple had to pass muster. A temple dedicated to the Lord had to be perfect. There was no room for sloppy work; hence the need for so many supervisors and highly skilled laborers.

Building a temple ninety feet long, thirty feet wide, and forty-five feet high took seven years. But the temple was a magnificent structure—a testament to a magnificent God. When the temple was finished and dedicated, Solomon made an offering appropriate for the occasion—22,000 cattle and 120,000 goats and sheep! And the sounds of celebrating during the fourteen-day festival were anything but quiet. Best of all, the glory of the Lord could be seen filling his new home on earth.

*This story is told in 2 Chronicles 2–3. To read the whole amazing story of this glorious temple, also read 2 Samuel 7; 1 Kings 5–8; and 1 Chronicles 22; 28–29.*

## Major Construction Projects in the Bible

| Project | Purpose | Reference |
|---|---|---|
| Tower of Babel | "Then they said, 'Come, let us build ourselves a city, with a tower that reaches to the heavens, so that we may make a name for ourselves and not be scattered over the face of the whole earth'" (NIV). | Genesis 11:1–8 |
| Tabernacle | "Then the Lord said to Moses: 'Set up the tabernacle, the Tent of Meeting, on the first day of the first month . . . Then the cloud covered the Tent of Meeting, and the glory of the Lord filled the tabernacle'" (NIV). | Exodus 35–40 |
| Solomon's Temple | "And so I [Solomon] intend to build a house for the name of the Lord my God, as the Lord said to David my father, 'Your son, whom I will set on your throne in your place, shall build the house for my name' . . . And when the priests came out of the Holy Place, a cloud filled the house of the Lord" (ESV). | 1 Kings 5–8; 2 Chronicles 2–5 |
| Solomon's Palace | "It took Solomon another thirteen years to finish building his own palace complex" (MSG). | 1 Kings 7:1–12 |
| Wall of Jerusalem | "The city where my ancestors are buried is in ruins, and the gates have been destroyed by fire. . . . So on October 2 the wall was finished—just fifty-two days after we had begun" (NLT). | Nehemiah 2:1–4:23, 6:1–7:3 |

# Extreme Makeover: Interior Edition

*Zerubbabel and Jeshua Start from the Inside Out While Renovating the Temple*

WE CAN'T HELP feeling nostalgic when we consider the way life used to be, especially when we see the ruins of a formerly grand building, one that played a key role in society. That's how the older generation felt in Jerusalem as they stood looking at the newly built altar and temple. But let's back up in the story.

The first temple built by Solomon was, hands down, the most important and the most beautiful building in ancient Jerusalem. The best materials were used to construct this house of God (check out "Under Construction," the story just before this). But when the army of Babylon invaded, nearly four hundred years after the construction of the temple, anything worth taking in the temple was snatched while the rest of it went up in flames (see 2 Kings 25).

After being exiled in Babylon, Ezra and thousands of other Israelites finally were allowed to make their way home to Jerusalem and towns in Judah. But the ruins of the temple in Jerusalem inspired more than just a feeling of nostalgia within them. Instead of sorrowing over the ruined temple, Jeshua, a priest, and Zerubbabel, the governor of Judah and the grandson of King Jehoiachin of Judah, were motivated. They decided to get God's house in order from the inside out, despite the opposition of those against the renovation.

But it took a kick in the pants from God, through the prophet Haggai, to actually get the building project started. (See "If You Build It, He Will Come," page 165.)

The first order of business was to build an altar where sacrifices could be offered to God. Since the altar was the premier object within the temple, this was the best way of establishing a firm spiritual foundation.

With the altar built, the people celebrated the Feast of Tabernacles in accordance with the law of Moses (see Leviticus 23:33–36). This feast was a reminder of the nomadic lifestyle of their people after the exodus. After this feast a system of regular sacrifices was put into practice.

Now that the people of Israel had their spiritual foundation well in hand, the time had come to lay the physical foundation of a new temple. As with the first temple, the people of Tyre and Sidon were solicited for cedar logs. Meanwhile Zerubbabel and Jeshua organized the construction, drafting Levites to help coordinate the building.

Once the foundation was set, the people celebrated. They sang the same praise refrain that had been sung during the first dedication of the temple, "praising and giving thanks to the Lord, saying 'For He is good, for His mercy and loving-kindness endure forever toward Israel'" (Ezra 3:11 AMP; see also 2 Chronicles 7:3).

But some of the people cried as they celebrated. They couldn't help remembering the old glorious temple. Sin had cost their nation grievously, but they had hope for a new beginning.

*To read more about the interior renovation of this second temple, which was known as Zerubbabel's temple, see Ezra 3.*

# Extreme Makeover: Exterior Edition

*Under Nehemiah's Leadership, the People Rebuild the Wall of Jerusalem in Fifty-two Days*

Factoids: Nehemiah
- *Domicile:* Jerusalem
- *Date:* Around 445 B.C.
- *Occupation:* Cupbearer to the king of Persia, then governor in Judah
- *Family Ties:* Father, Hecaliah
- *Mentioned in the Bible:* The book of Nehemiah

HOW MANY CONTRACTORS would be willing to take on a project such as rebuilding the wall around an entire city knowing that the due date would be in less than two months? A request such as that would get one of two responses—hysterical laughter or "Okay, but it's gonna cost ya!"

Nehemiah had a nice government job under the king of Persia. When he heard that the walls of his ancestral city were in disrepair, even crumbling in some places, he gave up his comfortable position to do what God asked him to do—rebuild the walls of Jerusalem.

From the moment he arrived in the city, everyone knew Nehemiah was in charge. He organized the people into groups and assigned each group a specific section of the wall. The third chapter in the book of Nehemiah takes us on a counterclockwise tour of each section of the city wall, describing the families, groups, and individuals who either rebuilt the walls or financed the project.

The first person mentioned is Eliashib, the high priest, who along with his fellow priests, pitched in and rebuilt the Sheep Gate and part of the walls nearby. These priests were not just spiritual leaders but men of action, leading by example. Then the list of laborers works its way from the northernmost gate—the Sheep Gate—around to the south, east, north, and west, back to the north gate. In a brilliant move, Nehemiah made the people responsible for repairing the section of wall nearest to their own house. He knew that the people would be more motivated to do the job well if it meant they were rebuilding the section that defended their own homes. This also allowed for entire families to pitch in, such as "Shallum . . . ruler of a half-district of Jerusalem" who "repaired the next section with the help of his daughters" (Nehemiah 3:12 NIV).

And, indeed, many hands made light work. Each little section in this enormous project had importance as the wall came together stone by stone. Through it all, Nehemiah's tenacity on this project is an example of good leadership and organization, as well as what can be accomplished when doing God's will. The people of Jerusalem followed Nehemiah's directions, and the wall was completed in fifty-two days (Nehemiah 6:15). What's more, when the enemies of Jerusalem "heard about this, all the surrounding nations were afraid and lost their self-confidence, because they realized that this work had been done with the help of . . . God" (6:16).

Nehemiah organized, managed, supervised, encouraged, dealt with slackers, and kept going until the walls were completed—proving he could hold his own against any contractor today.

*To read about all those who helped rebuild the walls of Jerusalem, read Nehemiah 3.*

# The Man
# Who Stunned Jesus

*A Roman Centurion Amazes Jesus with His Faith*

"I TELL YOU THE TRUTH, I have not found anyone in Israel with such great faith" (Matthew 8:10 NIV). To whom was Jesus referring in this statement? Surely it must have been one of his disciples, right? Or maybe someone whom he had just healed of some horrible and disfiguring disease? Or what about the adulterous woman he saved from stoning, or the Samaritan woman he spoke with at the well?

While Jesus did heal and help many and had many faithful Jewish disciples, he was not referring to any of those folks in this statement. He was speaking about a Roman centurion. He and this Roman army leader were separated by race, money, language, and social position, yet the centurion did not allow these differences to act as barriers. The centurion—a powerful man with means to get any help he needed—came to Jesus for help. That's the first big "wow."

He was on a mission to get aid for his servant and he knew Jesus was the only man who could help him. "Lord . . . my servant lies at home paralyzed and in terrible suffering" (8:6). When Jesus offered to go and heal the servant, the centurion humbly replied, "Lord, I do not deserve to have you come under my roof. But just say the word, and my servant will be healed" (8:8). Jesus was astounded by the man's answer!

Now, it's hard to believe that anything could stun and wow Jesus (who was God), but the Bible states it plainly: "When Jesus heard this, he was astonished" (8:10). He had never seen anyone in all of Israel with as much faith as this one Roman soldier. That's a second big "wow."

How could a Roman—a man hated by the Jews because his country oppressed and controlled them—have so much faith in Christ? This despised Gentile's faith put the Jewish religious leaders to shame. In fact, they were missing out on God's blessings because of their total lack of trust. They wouldn't believe Jesus really was who he said he was. How many miracles would it have taken for them to get the point? The Jews should have known the Messiah would come for everyone of all races, but they were too wrapped up in their own self-importance.

Jesus wasn't impressed with the self-righteous hoopla of the religious leaders. It took the simple faith of a humble man to really wow him.

*To read about the centurion's amazing faith, see Matthew 8:1–10.*

# An Equal Share

*Jesus Tells the Parable of the Laborers and Their Wages*

JESUS TOLD some great stories, but the parable about the laborers was a real mind twister. In effect, the story is that the guys hired late in the day were paid the same daily wage as the guys who were hired first thing that morning. So how did that pay scale break down, anyway?

Let's say the daily wage was a nice crisp twenty-dollar bill. The guys who walked in at 5:00 p.m. and worked for an hour got . . . twenty dollars. And the guys who worked all day in the hot sun also got . . . twenty dollars. Is that really fair?

Now, remember that this is a parable—a story that teaches a deeper truth. This particular parable really has nothing to do with hired workers and everything to do with how God's kingdom works. It's teaching us about grace, generously given by God.

Here's the story: A wealthy landowner went to the town square early in the morning. He was there to hire some workers to pick grapes in his vineyard, and he agreed to pay them a normal daily wage for their work. A few hours later, he realized his grapes weren't being picked fast enough, so he hired more workers. He did this a few more times throughout the day, culminating in a final hiring at the "eleventh hour," when the landowner asked a group of men, "Why haven't you been working today?" (Matthew 20:6 NLT). They said no one hired them, so he put them to work in his vineyard.

When evening came, the landowner told his foreman to call in the workers and pay them, beginning with the last workers first. So the foreman started giving out the twenty-dollar bills (actually, he was giving each man a denarius, the coin that typified a day's wage for a laborer).

He started by paying the men who were hired last. They each received a denarius. Then the men who had been hired earlier each received a denarius. Then in came the men who had worked from dawn to dusk, expecting to get paid a lot more, right? Wrong. They, too, received a denarius.

So they did what any of us might do—they complained. "Those people worked only one hour, and yet you've paid them just as much as you paid us who worked all day in the scorching heat" (20:12). They had worked all day long! Didn't they deserve more?

The master replied that he had not shortchanged them; in fact, he paid them exactly what they had agreed upon.

From this parable we learn that God's kingdom is not about getting an equal share or receiving what we deserve; but rather, it's about the wonder and power of undeserved grace and salvation. At the end of the day, none of us deserves that!

*Read the parable of the laborers and their wages in Matthew 20:1–16.*

# Pilate Procrastinates

*Pontius Pilate Can't Make Up His Mind About Jesus*

Factoids: Pontius Pilate
- *Domicile:* Caesarea
- *Date:* A.D. 30
- *Occupation:* Governor of Judea under the authority of Rome, A.D. 26–36
- *Family Ties:* Wife, unnamed
- *Mentioned in the Bible:* Matthew 27:11–26; Mark 15:1–15; Luke 23:1–25; John 18:28–19:16, 31, 38

WE'VE ALL KNOWN procrastinators and people-pleasers. Pilate, the Roman governor of Judea during the time of Jesus, was both. He will forever be known as the man who allowed Jesus to be crucified—a decision that he kept putting off.

Because the Romans controlled Palestine, the Jewish leaders did not have the authority to put a man to death. And Jesus, the man they considered an upstart and wished to see dead, had been arrested and tried before Caiaphas, the Jewish high priest, and the teachers of the law. Now it was the Roman governor's turn to question Jesus.

Jesus had had a rough night, having been questioned by the high priest and other Jewish leaders of the Sanhedrin—the Jewish council—most of the night. After being slapped and spit upon, he was tied up and dragged before Pilate in the manner of any other prisoner.

Pilate knew the Jewish leaders envied Jesus' popularity. He wanted to answer the accusation of the Jews—that Jesus claimed to be the king of his people in opposition to Rome. So he began the questioning with a simple one: "Are you the king of the Jews?" (Matthew 27:11 NIV).

Perhaps he expected a denial. But Jesus did not supply one. And what was more, Jesus did not answer his next questions, to Pilate's astonishment.

Watching the quiet man before him, Pilate couldn't help realizing that Jesus had committed no crime. He decided to put off the decision to execute Jesus by sending him to Herod Antipas, the tetrarch (the king of a quarter of the territory) of Galilee. But since Herod could find no fault in Jesus either (and couldn't get him to perform a miracle), he sent Jesus right back to Pilate.

During the night, Pilate's wife had a disturbing dream and sent a warning to Pilate. "Don't have anything to do with that innocent man" (27:19). If only he had listened. Instead, Pilate listened to the louder voices of the crowd who demanded Jesus' death.

Every year at Passover, Pilate released one prisoner. This year Pilate gave the people a choice of prisoners to release: he could release Barabbas, a man who had caused a riot and murdered someone; or he could release Jesus.

The mob made their choice clear: "Release Barabbas!" they yelled.

As for what was to be done with Jesus, again the crowd had an answer: "Crucify him!"

When Pilate still hesitated to give the word that would send Jesus to his death, the people pulled out the big-guns argument: "If you let this man go, you are no friend of Caesar. Anyone who claims to be a king opposes Caesar" (John 19:12).

So now Pilate was caught. The crowd wanted nothing less than execution. To try to clear his conscience, Pilate washed his hands as a symbol of washing his hands clean of shedding Jesus' blood. As far as he was concerned, the blood of the innocent man before him was now on their hands.

Jesus was handed over to be flogged and later crucified. Although Jesus came to earth to die for the sins of all, there were people along the way who made choices to help send him to his death. Pilate was one of them. He put off doing the right thing to save his reputation. Ultimately, it cost him his soul.

*To read more about Pilate's indecision, read Matthew 27:11–26; Mark 15:1–15; Luke 23:1–25; and John 18:28–19:16.*

# A Labor of Love

*Friends of a Paralyzed Man Lower Him Through a Roof*

WHEN YOU SEE someone in need, what is your response? Do you approach God in prayer for the person in distress? Are you a person of action who jumps right in to help?

A group of men in the town of Capernaum were men of action and great faith. Jesus had returned to his home, and so many people gathered to hear him preach that it was standing room only—inside and outside the house.

Onto this scene arrive some men carrying a rather unique package—another man, lying on a mat. We know there were at least four of them because Scripture tells us that "some men came, bringing to him a paralytic, carried by four of them" (Mark 2:3 NIV). Perhaps there were eight or twelve all together, allowing shifts while carrying their friend what might have been many miles. Although Scripture doesn't tell us much about them, we know these three things:

1. These men were the best friends a guy could have. How many people do you know who would be willing take time out of their busy schedules and carry/drive someone with severe needs a long distance to get help? Probably not too many, right? This paralyzed man had a whole group of friends who were willing to give up their plans to help him.

2. Not only were they great friends, they had great faith. These men had heard of Jesus and of his power to heal. They believed

Jesus would restore their friend and they didn't hesitate to seek out the Great Physician.

3. These men were persistent. "Since they could not get him to Jesus because of the crowd, they made an opening in the roof above Jesus and, after digging through it, lowered the mat the paralyzed man was lying on" (2:4). Houses in Bible times were usually constructed of stone, but the roof would have been made of mud and straw. Can't you just see the men clawing and tearing at the roof while Jesus preached in the house below? The people inside the house must have been perplexed when pieces of roof began pelting them in the head! Then finally, when the hole was big enough, they lowered their friend down into the midst of the crowd around Jesus.

When Jesus saw the faith of the paralyzed man and his friends, he said, "Son, your sins are forgiven. . . . get up, take your mat and go home" (2:5, 11). And what happened? "He got up, took his mat and walked out in full view of them all" (2:12).

What joy those men must have felt as they clapped their friend on the back and *walked* home with him. While everyone else stood by in amazement, these men realized that Jesus had acknowledged their faith and answered their unspoken request for their friend. Of course, we also hope that they put the roof back together before they left!

*Read the account of the paralyzed man in Mark 2:1–12. The story is also recorded in Matthew 9:1–8 and Luke 5:17–26.*

# A Brother in Arms

*Jesus' Brother James Becomes a Leader of the Church*

Factoids: James, brother of Jesus
- *Domicile:* Grew up with Jesus in Nazareth
- *Date:* Lived in the first century A.D.
- *Occupation:* After believing, became leader of Jerusalem church
- *Family Ties:* Father, Joseph; mother, Mary; brothers, Jesus, Jude, and others
- *Mentioned in the Bible:* Matthew 13:55; Mark 6:3; John 7:5; Acts 12:17; 15:13; 21:18; 1 Corinthians 15:7; Galatians 1:19; 2:9; the book of James

IT'S SOMETIMES HARDEST to prove ourselves to our family and close friends. They know our strengths and weaknesses. Worst of all, they remember the embarrassing nicknames we had as children.

Whether or not Jesus had nicknames among his siblings, the fact remains that at one point his family did not believe he was the promised Messiah. After being rejected in Nazareth, Jesus told the crowd, "A prophet is not without honor except in his hometown, among his relatives, and in his household" (Mark 6:4 HCSB). How well he knew the truth of this statement, as was seen at the next Feast of Tabernacles.

The Feast of Tabernacles was a celebration of God's provision during Israel's time in the wilderness after the Exodus. During this festival, many traveled to Jerusalem and lived in temporary shelters, just as the Israelites had done during the forty years of wandering in the wilderness. Jesus was planning to celebrate the festival, but waited for just the right time to go. During his years of ministry, he made enemies—enemies who sought to take his life.

Jesus' brothers, including James, wondered why he hesitated about going up to the feast. They couldn't understand this strange brother of theirs, and they offered their two cents' worth of advice in a tone of mockery: "Leave here and go to Judea, so that your disciples also may see the works you are doing. For no one works in secret if he seeks to be known openly. If you do these things, show yourself to the world" (John 7:3–4 ESV).

Imagine being so close to Jesus and not realizing who he was. The saying "familiarity breeds contempt" was true in this instance. But Jesus went to the feast on his own timetable—not theirs.

Later on, at some point after Jesus' resurrection, James became a believer. He was there in Jerusalem with the other disciples waiting for the coming of the Holy Spirit, and he became one of the pillars of the early church.

In his letter to the believers in Galatia, Paul later referred to James as one of the apostles—one of the leaders empowered to care for the needs of believers within the growing church. (See Galatians 1:19.) James served on the council when Paul and Barnabas met with the leaders to determine whether or not Gentile believers needed to follow the circumcision law. He argued against "majoring on the minors," and advocated making it easier for Gentiles to become followers of Jesus. (See Acts 15:12–21.)

James had a true overhaul regarding Jesus' identity as the Messiah. Although he started off mocking Jesus, he lived the rest of his life knowing that Jesus—his brother—died to save him. He was truly a brother in arms—a fellow soldier in the cause of Christ.

*To learn more about this amazing brother of Christ, read John 7:1–10; Acts 15:13–21; and the book of James.*

# A Pearl
# Among the Poor

*Dorcas, aka Tabitha, Leads the Field in Kindness*

S OME LEADERS are known for their quotable quotes that inspire, such as John F. Kennedy's "Ask not what your country can do for you; ask what you can do for your country." Other leaders are known for their philanthropy, giving huge quantities of money to good causes. But sometimes a leader is someone we least suspect . . . like the girl next door. Such was Tabitha (also known as Dorcas), a believer living in the town of Joppa during the first century. She was a leader in her own right: she led her community in kindness and service.

One day Dorcas became ill and died, to the deep sadness of all who knew her. A fitting epitaph for her life comes through the text: "She was always doing good works and acts of charity" (Acts 9:36 HCSB). Her friends (mainly widows) had the sad duty of preparing her body for burial. While death is normally the end of the road, an unexpected fork appeared in this case.

Some disciples in Joppa learned that the apostle Peter was in a town nearby (Lydda), and asked him to drop by. After all, Peter had performed a miracle or two in his day, thanks to the power of the Holy Spirit (see Acts 3). In fact, upon arriving in Lydda, the former fisherman healed Aeneas, a paralyzed man.

When Peter arrived at the room where Dorcas had been placed, the widows showed him the fruit of her labor—clothes she had made and given away to those in need.

Peter asked the mourners to leave the room. Then he knelt and prayed—a move reminiscent of his Master, Jesus, and the great prophet Elijah. After praying, Peter spoke a simple command, using her Aramaic name: "Tabitha, get up!" (Acts 9:40). And she did!

Like the child raised by Elijah (see 1 Kings 17:22), the dead returned to life. One wonders what went through Tabitha's mind when she woke up. Peter showed her to the mourners who had gathered—mourners now turned into rejoicers! As the news of Dorcas's return to life spread throughout the region, many people became followers of Jesus Christ.

This miracle wasn't about Peter's ability to raise the dead. It was about turning people's hearts toward Jesus. Perhaps Dorcas's miracle inspired others toward even greater acts of kindness. If so, she was back to lead the way.

*To read more about Dorcas and her gifts of kindness, see Acts 9:32–42.*

# A Voice to the Gentiles

*Peter Changes His Tune in Regard to the Gentiles*

Factoids: Peter
- *Domicile:* From Bethsaida, in the region of Galilee
- *Date:* First century A.D.

- *Occupation:* Fisherman, disciple
- *Family Ties:* Father, John; brother, Andrew; wife, unnamed
- *Mentioned in the Bible:* Gospels; Acts; Galatians 1:18; 2:7–14; 1 and 2 Peter

THE EARLY CHURCH was initially made up of Jews who followed Jesus Christ. Many of these believers thought the church should only be for Jewish folks. But God was about to challenge that idea, and he used Peter to do it.

There was a centurion named Cornelius who lived in Caesarea. Cornelius was not your usual run-of-the-mill Roman centurion. Rather, he was known for his generosity and for his prayer habits. His whole household worshipped God. Obviously God was pleased with him, because one afternoon during his regular prayer time, an angel appeared and called his name.

Frightened by the sudden appearance of the angel, Cornelius didn't know what to make of this being. But the angel had good news: "Your prayers and gifts to the poor have come up as a memorial offering before God. Now send men to Joppa to bring back a man named Simon who is called Peter. He is staying with Simon the tanner, whose house is by the sea" (Acts 10:4–6 NIV).

Cornelius didn't waste time debating about whether or not he should obey. He sent a trusted soldier and some servants to find this man called Peter.

Meanwhile, in Joppa, God was preparing the apostle Peter for something he never would have dreamed could happen. While praying up on the roof of the house one afternoon, Peter saw a vision of a large sheet that held all sorts of animals, some of which were unclean according to Jewish dietary laws. After hearing a voice telling him to kill and eat whatever he found on the sheet, Peter refused. Hadn't he always abided by the kosher laws? Good Jews never ate things that were unclean.

But the voice replied with words that undoubtedly stunned Peter's sensibilities: "When God says that something can be used for food, don't say it isn't fit to eat" (10:15 CEV).

About the same time, Cornelius's representatives arrived where Peter was staying and asked to see him. Peter was still trying to figure out what the vision meant when the Holy Spirit told him to go with the people at the door. Peter obeyed, taking some of the believers from Joppa with him to the home of Cornelius.

Entering the home of a Gentile was a momentous occasion for Peter, a Jew, for it meant going against the laws and traditions with which he had grown up. Cornelius invited his friends and relatives to come and meet the celebrity—Peter. After stories were exchanged, Peter finally got the message of this momentous visit and his vision. "I now realize how true it is that God does not show favoritism but accepts men from every nation who fear him and do what is right" (10:34–35 NIV).

Then Peter went on to do what he probably never imagined he would do: he shared the gospel with Gentiles! Sensing the presence of the Holy Spirit, Peter suggested that Cornelius and those in his household be baptized. What joy there was in the home of Cornelius that day. Gentiles were a part of God's family now.

*To read more about Cornelius and Peter, see Acts 10.*

## KINGS OF ISRAEL AND JUDAH

### KINGS OF ISRAEL

| KING | DATES | LENGTH OF REIGN | CHARACTER | REFERENCES |
|------|-------|-----------------|-----------|------------|
| Jeroboam I | 930–909 B.C. | 22 years | Evil | 1 Kings 11:26–14:34; 2 Chronicles 10:12–13:20 |
| Nadab | 909–908 B.C. | 2 years | Evil | 1 Kings 15:25–28 |

| KING | DATES | LENGTH OF REIGN | CHARACTER | REFERENCES |
|------|-------|-----------------|-----------|------------|
| Baasha | 908–886 B.C. | 24 years | Evil | 1 Kings 15:27–16:7; 2 Chronicles 16:1–6 |
| Elah | 886–885 B.C. | 2 years | Evil | 1 Kings 16:6–14 |
| Zimri | 885 B.C. | 7 days | Evil | 1 Kings 16:9–20 |
| Tibni | 885 B.C. | Unknown (short) | Evil | 1 Kings 16:21–22 |
| Omri | 885–874 B.C. | 12 years | Evil | 1 Kings 16:16–28 |
| Ahab | 874–853 B.C. | 22 years | Evil | 1 Kings 16:28–22:40; 2 Chronicles 18:1–34 |
| Ahaziah | 853–852 B.C. | 2 years | Evil | 1 Kings 22:40– 2 Kings 1:18 2 Chronicles 20:35–37 |
| Joram | 852–841 B.C. | 12 years | Evil | 2 Kings 3:1–8:25; 2 Chronicles 22:5–7 |
| Jehu | 841–814 B.C. | 28 years | Evil | 2 Kings 9:1–10:36; 2 Chronicles 22:7–12 |
| Jehoahaz | 814–798 B.C. | 17 years | Evil | 2 Kings 13:1–9 |
| Jehoash | 798–793 B.C. | 16 years | Evil | 2 Kings 13:10–14:16; 2 Chronicles 25:17–24 |
| Jeroboam II | 793–753 B.C. | 41 years | Evil | 2 Kings 14:16–29 |

| KING | DATES | LENGTH OF REIGN | CHARACTER | REFERENCES |
|------|-------|-----------------|-----------|------------|
| Zechariah | 753–752 B.C. | 6 months | Evil | 2 Kings 14:29–15:11 |
| Shallum | 752 B.C. | 1 month | Evil | 2 Kings 15:10–15 |
| Menahem | 752–742 B.C. | 10 years | Evil | 2 Kings 15:14–22 |
| Pekahiah | 742–740 B.C. | 2 years | Evil | 2 Kings 15:22–26 |
| Pekah | 740–732 B.C. | 8 years | Evil | 2 Kings 15:25–31; 2 Chronicles 28:5–8 |
| Hoshea | 732–724 B.C. | 9 years | Evil | 2 Kings 15:30; 17:1–6 |

## KINGS OF JUDAH

| KING | DATES | LENGTH OF REIGN | CHARACTER | REFERENCES |
|------|-------|-----------------|-----------|------------|
| Rehoboam | 930–913 B.C. | 17 years | Evil | 1 Kings 11:43–14:31; 2 Chronicles 9:31–12:16 |
| Abijah | 913–910 B.C. | 3 years | Evil | 1 Kings 14:31–15:8; 2 Chronicles 13:1–14:1 |
| Asa | 910–870 B.C. | 41 years | Good | 1 Kings 15:8–24; 2 Chronicles 14:1–16:14 |
| Jehoshaphat | 872–847 B.C. | 25 years | Good | 1 Kings 15:24; 22:41–50; 2 Chronicles 17:1–21:1 |

| KING | DATES | LENGTH OF REIGN | CHARACTER | REFERENCES |
|------|-------|-----------------|-----------|------------|
| Jehoram | 848–841 B.C. | 8 years | Evil | 2 Kings 8:16–24; 2 Chronicles 21:1–20 |
| Ahaziah | 841 B.C. | 1 year | Evil | 2 Kings 8:24–9:29; 2 Chronicles 22:1–10 |
| Athaliah (Queen) | 841–835 B.C. | 6 years | Evil | 2 Kings 11:1–20; 2 Chronicles 22:10–23:21 |
| Joash | 835–796 B.C. | 40 years | Good | 2 Kings 11:2–12:21; 2 Chronicles 22:11–24:27 |
| Amaziah | 796–767 B.C. | 29 years | Good | 2 Kings 14:1–20; 2 Chronicles 25:1–28 |
| Azariah (aka Uzziah) | 792–767 B.C. (coreign) and 767–740 B.C. | 52 years | Good | 2 Kings 15:1–17; 2 Chronicles 26:1–23 |
| Jotham | 750–740 B.C. (coreign) and 740–732 B.C. | 16 years | Good | 2 Kings 15:32–38; 2 Chronicles 27:1–9 |
| Ahaz | 735–732 B.C. (coreign) and 732–715 B.C. | 16 years | Evil | 2 Kings 16:1–20; 2 Chronicles 28:1–27 |
| Hezekiah | 715–699 B.C. | 29 years | Good | 2 Kings 16:20; 18:1–20:21 2 Chronicles 29:1–32:33 |

| KING | DATES | LENGTH OF REIGN | CHARACTER | REFERENCES |
|------|-------|-----------------|-----------|------------|
| Manasseh | 697–642 B.C. | 55 years | Evil (but repented at the end) | 2 Kings 21:1–18; 2 Chronicles 33:1–20 |
| Amon | 642–640 B.C. | 2 years | Evil | 2 Kings 21:18–26; 2 Chronicles 33:20–25 |
| Josiah | 640–609 B.C. | 31 years | Good | 2 Kings 21:26–23:30; 2 Chronicles 33:25–35:27 |
| Jehoahaz | 609 B.C. | 3 months | Evil | 2 Kings 23:30–34; 2 Chronicles 36:1–4 |
| Jehoiakim | 609–598 B.C. | 11 years | Evil | 2 Kings 23:34–24:6; 2 Chronicles 36:5–8 |
| Jehoiachin | 598 B.C. | 3 months | Evil | 2 Kings 24:6–15; 25:27–30; 2 Chronicles 36:8–10 |
| Zedekiah | 597–586 B.C. | 11 years | Evil | 2 Kings 24:17–25:21; 2 Chronicles 36:10–21 |

# PART FOUR

# Prophets and Losses

# The Prophet
# and the Pharaoh

*Moses Takes On the Mighty Pharaoh*

Factoids: Moses
- *Domicile:* Egypt, then the wilderness as he led the Hebrew people
- *Date:* Around 1350 to 1240 B.C.
- *Occupation:* Prince, shepherd, national leader
- *Family Ties:* Brother, Aaron; sister, Miriam; wife, Zipporah; sons, Gershom and Eliezer
- *Mentioned in the Bible:* The books of Exodus, Leviticus, Numbers, and Deuteronomy tell his story; he is mentioned throughout Scripture because of his importance to the nation's history; see also Acts 7:20–44; Hebrews 11:23–29

IT MIGHT HAVE been funny if it weren't such a serious situation. Mighty Pharaoh, leader of the powerful nation of Egypt, was brought to his knees by the shepherd from the backside of the wilderness.

But that's getting ahead of the story.

The Hebrew people had settled in Egypt when Joseph was second-in-command. (Read about that in Genesis 46.) Many years had passed and the new pharaoh didn't care about Joseph and his heritage. All the current pharaoh saw were millions of people, enough to make a pretty powerful army should they attempt to rebel against Egypt. So he decided to force the Hebrews into slavery. Eventually, even a command was sent out to kill all Hebrew boys at birth so that fewer strong men could rise up against Egypt. (You can read that horrendous story in "Death on the Nile," page 77.)

You know the basics of the Moses story: He was placed in a basket as a baby on the Nile River, pulled from the river by Pharaoh's daughter, and raised in the palace, yet nursed and cared for by his own mother. (See Exodus 1–2.) Apparently he had been taught well by his mother, because he later became concerned about the plight of his native people who faced such harsh slavery conditions. At one point, when he saw an Egyptian mistreating a Hebrew slave, Moses killed the Egyptian, and the man had to run for his life into the desert.

Enter the burning bush (so to speak). After forty years as a shepherd in the desert, Moses had a "near-bush" experience. From the burning bush, God spoke to Moses and sent him back to Egypt from whence he had come. His task? "I am sending you to Pharaoh to bring my people the Israelites out of Egypt" (Exodus 3:10 NIV).

Say what?

But Moses had heard right the first time. After some back and forth with the bush (and God), Moses and his brother Aaron grabbed their shepherd staffs and began the long trek across the wilderness and back to the big city.

Let's face it. These guys looked like nothing more than country bumpkins. They surely caused a stir when they walked the streets toward the pharaoh's palace. What could they possibly want with the pharaoh?

Easy. Just the freedom of well over a million people (the Bible says there were "six hundred thousand men . . . besides women and children," 12:37). Their message was straight from the bush (and God): "Let my people go" (5:1).

Ah, but Pharaoh was not so easily convinced. This was slave labor they were talking about—a nation of people building beautiful cities at no charge! They couldn't go on strike. They couldn't hold out for higher wages or better conditions. They just kept right on building buildings. Why in the world would he let them go?

Because, said Moses, "This is what the LORD, the God of Israel says" (5:1).

Pharaoh looked at the two ragtag men in front of him. Then he gazed out across his veranda at the massive numbers of slaves crawling like ants around the latest building project. *Yeah, sure. The god of these people is surely a god to be afraid of. Ooooh, I'd better hurry up and follow this god's instructions. Yeah, right.*

So Pharaoh did what any self-respecting, all-powerful leader would do. He kicked them out.

But then God began a process of humiliating the many gods of Egypt that Pharaoh *did* respect. He took on Hapi and Anuket, the god and goddess of the Nile River, and turned the river to blood (7:14–24). He showed the powerlessness of Heqet, the frog goddess, as frogs came up out of the Nile and filled the homes of the Egyptians (8:1–15). Then came plagues of gnats, flies, killing of livestock, boils, hail, and locusts (8:16–10:20). God faced down Re, the sun god, by causing darkness to descend on all of Egypt except where the Hebrews lived (10:21–29). Through it all, God was making the point that all of Egypt's "protector gods" had no power at all.

But Pharaoh still wouldn't budge. Not, that is, until the final plague descended, killing all the firstborn sons—including Pharaoh's firstborn and heir to the throne (11:1–12:33). Only then did Pharaoh listen. In despair, he sent the Hebrew people on their way.

But wait! There's more.

After the millions of people left town, Pharaoh suddenly realized what he had done. So, taking his army, he took off after the slaves to bring them back to work.

God still had a trick up his sleeve. The Hebrews appeared to be trapped, with the Red Sea in front of them and Pharaoh's army closing in behind. God opened the waters to let his people walk directly through the sea. Then he dropped the waters onto Pharaoh's army! And that was the end of that.

*For all the gnatty, dark details of Moses's run-in with Pharaoh, read Exodus 5–14.*

# A Royal Pain

*Samuel Anoints—and Rebukes—Israel's First King*

Factoids: Samuel
- *Domicile:* Ramathaim, in the hill country of Ephraim
- *Date:* Around 1100 B.C.
- *Occupation:* Judge, prophet, priest
- *Family Ties:* Father, Elkanah; mother, Hannah; sons, Joel and Abiah
- *Mentioned in the Bible:* 1 Samuel 1–28; Psalm 99:6; Jeremiah 15:1; Acts 3:24; 13:20; Hebrews 11:32

THIS IS A TALE OF TWO LEADERS, one far more bizarre than anything Charles Dickens could have imagined. It began with a voice calling out in the night—a call leading to Samuel's multitasking job as prophet, judge, kingmaker and, ultimately, king breaker.

Born to a barren woman who battered the doors of heaven with her pleas for a son (see 1 Samuel 1), baby Samuel became the gift returned to the giver with gratitude. His mother, Hannah, gave him back to God, promising that her son would serve God. And serve God he did.

God often made himself known in unexpected ways to the people he chose as prophets. He used a bush to call Moses (Exodus 3) and a vision of a king on a throne to call Isaiah (Isaiah 6). Samuel was chosen not only as a prophet but also as a judge of the people of Israel (1 Samuel 3 and 7). Back in Samuel's day, the judge was the ultimate leader and arbiter of the people—God's agent of change. He joined a long line of judges such as Othniel, Ehud, Deborah, Gideon, Jephthah, and the most infamous judge of all—Samson. We may equate being a judge with being a Supreme Court justice and a military general, while a prophet acted as national security adviser and secretary of state all rolled into one. After a long history of judges, Samuel had the distinction of being the last judge of Israel. A change was in the wind.

While God was satisfied with Samuel as his spokesperson, his people weren't satisfied with being led by the elderly Samuel and his less-than-reputable sons. The people wanted a monarchy, like all the other nations had. But God saw through their request. What they were really saying was, "We don't want to be led by God. We want a leader in our image—a leader with some skin."

Samuel warned the people what having a king would involve. "He will take your sons and make them serve with his chariots and horses, and they will run in front of his chariots. . . . He will take a tenth of your flocks, and you yourselves will become his slaves. When that day comes, you will cry out for relief from the king you have chosen, and the LORD will not answer you in that day" (1 Samuel 8:10, 17–18 NIV).

Of course the people didn't listen, so enamored were they with the idea of having a king. So Samuel's next task was to find the king. Once the king was chosen—a process involving lots rather than votes—Samuel's position would be strictly that of national security adviser and priest.

God gave the people exactly what they wanted by choosing Saul, from the tribe of Benjamin. Saul fit the profile perfectly. He was tall and good-looking and came from a good family of wealth and influence—just the way we all like our leaders. Undoubtedly he provided a marked contrast to the elderly Samuel. Saul didn't have to hit the campaign trail, kiss babies, debate other candidates, or write a book including his innermost thoughts. All he had to do was be anointed by Samuel, then Saul was good to go. The new age of the kings had begun.

Saul became king at the age of thirty and spent more than four decades in that position. While he looked the part on the outside, he had a tendency to blow it, like any fallible human being. During a time of war with the Philistines, Saul arrogantly decided to ignore Samuel's instructions to wait for him to offer the burnt offering, and instead did it himself (read "Only Fools Rush In," page 223). As a consequence, the Lord revealed to Samuel that Saul's kingship would end. So much for tenure.

We may shake our heads and wonder whether Saul's actions were so heinous. After all, in other places we read of kings like David and Solomon who offered burnt offerings to the Lord. The problem with Saul was his disobedience. Rejecting Samuel's instructions was akin to rejecting God's. The final straw came during a battle with the Amalekites, when Saul disobeyed a direct order from God to "destroy everything that belongs to them" (15:3). Saul couldn't bring himself to do that, and the Lord rejected Saul as king.

There's a sad moral to the story that we can't help noticing. God sometimes gives us what we want only to show us that what we want isn't worth having.

*To read more about Samuel and Saul, see 1 Samuel 3, 7, and 12–15.*

# A "Tear"-ible Thing

*Ahijah Tears Up His Cloak to Signify the End of the United Kingdom of Israel*

SOMETIMES BEING WISE doesn't necessarily mean being smart. King Solomon had it all. He presided over the golden age of the nation of Israel. His nation was prosperous and at peace—mainly due to the hard work of his warrior father, King David, who had subdued Israel's enemies. The groundwork of a strong kingdom was laid before Solomon took the throne.

God had promised King David that one of his descendants would always reign (a prophecy ultimately fulfilled in Jesus Christ, who came from David's line, but also fulfilled in the birth of his son Solomon, chosen by God to be Israel's king after David's death). After Solomon took the throne, God said he could ask for whatever he wanted, and Solomon prayed, "Give your servant therefore an understanding mind to govern your people, that I may discern between good and evil, for who is able to govern this your great people?" (1 Kings 3:9 ESV).

So far so good.

Solomon ruled well, was renowned for his wisdom, built God's temple, wrote all kinds of books (such as Proverbs, Ecclesiastes, and the Song of Songs), married all kinds of women . . .

Oops. Not so good.

Seems that having a peaceful kingdom allowed Solomon time to get himself into trouble. And that he did. Solomon allowed himself to be drawn into the worship of other gods. And with seven hundred wives and concubines to keep happy (1 Kings 11:3), Solomon apparently was kept busy building high places for them to worship.

The result? God was angry—really, really angry with Solomon. And when God is ticked, "tear"-ible things happen.

One night Solomon apparently got another visit from God, who told him: "Since this has been your practice and you have not kept my covenant and my statutes that I have commanded you, I will surely tear the kingdom from you and will give it to your servant" (11:11).

Enter the prophet Ahijah.

Given a word from the Lord, Ahijah dutifully met up with a man named Jeroboam as he was leaving the city of Jerusalem one day. Jeroboam was one of King Solomon's officials, apparently a hardworking, trustworthy man (11:26–28). As Ahijah and Jeroboam stood alone on a country road, Ahijah took off his new cloak and tore it into twelve pieces—each piece symbolizing one of the twelve tribes of Israel. Handing ten pieces to Jeroboam, he gave this prophecy from God: "Take for yourself ten pieces, for thus says the LORD, the God of Israel, 'Behold, I am about to tear the kingdom from the hand of Solomon and will give you ten tribes'" (11:31). Solomon's son would keep one tribe (actually, two tribes, Judah and Benjamin—but Benjamin was the smallest tribe and bordered Judah, so the two were spoken of as one). God left Solomon's line one tribe, "for the sake of David my servant whom I chose, who kept my commandments and my statutes" (11:34).

At that moment a new chapter began in the history of Israel as a nation. The united kingdom of Israel became a divided kingdom. The northern kingdom, which continued to be called Israel, had Jeroboam as its first king, and the capital city was first at Shechem and then farther north in Samaria. The southern kingdom was called Judah after the largest tribe, had Rehoboam (Solomon's son) as its first king, and the capital city was at Jerusalem.

It might not have been so "tear"-ible if Rehoboam and Jeroboam had been obedient to God, but, sadly, that was not the case. You can read about that in "North versus South" on page 50.

*Ahijah's "tear"-ible prophecy is in 1 Kings 11:26–40.*

# A Thorn in Their Side

*Elijah Confronts the Wrongs of Ahab and Jezebel*

SOME PEOPLE are a constant source of friction. Their presence rubs others the wrong way. They're like a splinter in the finger or a thorn in the side. But some people can be irritating simply because they take a stand for what's right. Elijah stood for what was right. He was God's man in a turbulent time.

Ahab was one of the most disobedient kings in Israel's history—something he learned from his father, Omri. His tendency to disobey God was apparent in his choice of a wife. Jezebel was a daughter of the Sidonian king and a Baal worshipper. Ahab even built altars where sacrifices to Baal could be offered.

Whenever disobedience reared its ugly head, God sent a prophet to warn the people. This time he sent Elijah, a man from Tishbe, setting the stage for one of the most confrontational relationships in Bible history, and one that lasted for years.

Round one came when Elijah warned Ahab that God would withhold rain for the next three years. Boom! A direct hit against Baal, the alleged god of fertility and rain clouds. But during the drought, God provided for Elijah by having ravens bring food twice a day. He then sent Elijah to Zarephath, where he instructed a widow to provide food for Elijah (see 1 Kings 17).

Round two was a contest on Mount Carmel involving 450 prophets of Baal, 400 prophets of Asherah (another false god worshipped by Jezebel), and the Lord. Whichever god answered by fire would be the true God. By this time, Elijah wanted the people of Israel to stop going back and forth between worshipping the true God and worshipping Baal.

This was indeed the greatest show on earth. Everyone showed up on Mount Carmel as instructed. After the 850 screaming prophets called on their gods all day to no avail, God proved victorious by sending fire to burn a water-drenched sacrifice. After the Baal/Asherah prophets were killed at Elijah's command, God sent rain (see 1 Kings 18).

In round three, a determined Jezebel came up swinging, vowing to have Elijah killed. She was a little steamed about the deaths of her prophets. A discouraged Elijah escaped and was encouraged by God. Elijah even learned the identity of his successor—Elisha (see 1 Kings 19 and "Extreme Exit—Part 2," page 21).

Round four involved Ahab's desire to have the vineyard of his neighbor, Naboth. But Naboth refused to sell his land to Ahab. So he went home to whine to Jezebel (see "Whining over a Winery," page 18). Jezebel framed Naboth for a crime he didn't commit, which led to his being stoned to death, and Ahab claimed the vineyard. But the God who saw all sent Elijah to confront Ahab about the murder and theft. He prophesied that not only would Ahab die, Jezebel would die as well. "In the place where dogs licked up the blood of Naboth shall dogs lick your own blood. . . . The dogs shall eat Jezebel within the walls of Jezreel" (1 Kings 21:19, 23 ESV).

Oddly enough, Ahab repented. God relented and said he would not bring doom during Ahab's lifetime, but Ahab's son would feel the full force of God's judgment. Both Ahab and Jezebel died and their deaths happened exactly as Elijah had prophesied.

It just goes to show that when God's man gets in the ring, he can KO anyone.

*To read more about Elijah, Ahab, and Jezebel, check out 1 Kings 16:29–21:28.*

# The Bearer
# of Bad News

*Micaiah's No in the Face of Four Hundred Yeses Angers King Ahab*

MANY KINGS IN HISTORY have surrounded themselves with yes-men—sycophants who tell them exactly what they want to hear. But a true prophet of God was supposed to be above that sort of thing when counseling a king. He was to speak only the words God gave him to speak. So when four hundred prophets said yes to two kings, and only one prophet said no, discerning the truth became a little dicey.

In the divided kingdom of Israel, Jehoshaphat was king of Judah (the southern kingdom) and Ahab was king of Israel (the northern kingdom). When Ahab suggested that the two halves of the kingdom join forces against the Arameans, Jehoshaphat reminded Ahab to "first seek the counsel of the LORD" (1 Kings 22:5 NIV).

So Ahab gathered together his best group of four hundred prophets. (Amazing, after the PR damage that was done to his prophets on Mount Carmel—see 1 Kings 18:16–40.) All these guys had only good news for Ahab: If the kings went to war, God would assure their victory.

Ahab must have smiled to himself. These prophets told him exactly what he wanted to hear. How unlike his dealings with Elijah—God's man at Mount Carmel and in Naboth's vineyard (1 Kings 21)—who seemed to have been born to oppose Ahab.

There was something about the word from the "yes" prophets that didn't sit well with Jehoshaphat, though. Surely there had to be someone else who could offer advice.

Perhaps Ahab groaned as he recounted the one prophet who "never prophesies anything good about me, but always bad" (22:8). This wasn't Elijah, however. The prophet he referred to was Micaiah son of Imlah.

After being counseled to agree with what the four hundred prophets said, Micaiah instead replied, "As surely as the Lord lives, I can tell him only what the Lord tells me" (22:14).

When face-to-face with the two kings, Micaiah provided a sarcastic agreement, as if acknowledging, "This is what you want to hear, King Ahab."

Ahab recognized the sarcasm and demanded a real answer. How ironic. But the real answer was a chilling one.

Micaiah then told a story with God's throne room in heaven as the setting. Through the story, Micaiah explained that God allowed a lying spirit to speak through the prophets who agreed with Ahab's plan of war. Ahab would die in battle, because the Lord was not with him.

Well, Zedekiah, one of the four hundred prophets, was not about to take this accusation lying down. He retaliated by slapping and mocking Micaiah. But he couldn't stop Micaiah's words from coming true.

While Micaiah was thrown in prison for speaking the truth, the kings went to war. But even after disguising himself, an arrow found King Ahab. Death came just as Micaiah predicted.

Micaiah was willing to be the bearer of bad news in defiance of the crowd. In his case, bad news was actually good advice.

*Read about Ahab and his "no man" Micaiah in 1 Kings 22:1–39.*

# The Glamour of Greed

*Elisha's Godly Example Shows Up Gehazi's Greed*

Factoids: Elisha
- *Domicile:* Northern kingdom (Israel)
- *Date:* Around 840 B.C.
- *Occupation:* Farmer, prophet
- *Family Ties:* Father, Shaphat
- *Mentioned in the Bible:* 1 Kings 19:16–21; 2 Kings 2:1–13:20; Luke 4:27

A JOB WELL DONE is worth a reward, isn't it? Elisha, one of the most effective prophets in the Old Testament, would say no. Elisha's servant Gehazi would disagree with him.

Gehazi was probably one of the disciples of Elisha who helped him with everyday tasks in return for his education. He just happened to be with Elisha when God called upon the prophet to heal an Aramean officer named Naaman.

Naaman was a great military hero who had been stricken with a dreaded disease: leprosy. Having learned from a servant girl that a prophet of God existed in Israel, Naaman traveled to the king of Israel with a letter from his own king requesting healing for Naaman. Elisha soon discovered Naaman's plight and told the seeking general to wash in the Jordan River seven times. On the final time he would be healed.

Naaman was none too thrilled at the thought of dipping himself in the dirty waters of the Jordan, but in the end, he humbled himself and did as Elisha directed. "And his flesh was restored and became clean like that of a young boy" (2 Kings 5:14 NIV).

Naaman stood before Elisha and said, "Now I know that there is no God in all the world except in Israel" (5:15). He was so grateful to God for his miraculous cure that he offered Elisha a reward for healing him. But Elisha refused the gifts, knowing that the Lord was responsible for Naaman's healing.

And what should have been the end of the story was only the beginning. Gehazi must have thought that Naaman got off too easily. After all, he was a rich and powerful man who had just been given a miracle—why shouldn't he have to pay something?

He hurried after Naaman with a scheme already in mind to gain the rewards Elisha had rejected: two talents of silver and two sets of clothing. Unfortunately, there were three problems with his scheme: First, he lied to Naaman about why he needed the money and clothing. Second, he implied that God's miracles could be purchased. And third, he hid the clothing and money, then lied to Elisha upon his return.

When questioned by Elisha, Gehazi lied to the prophet of God. As a result, he was stricken with the disease of which Naaman had been healed, and his descendants ended up suffering as well.

At one point, Gehazi had been a faithful servant focused upon learning about God and serving his master. However, when the opportunity presented itself, greed held more glamour than serving God.

Elisha was a prophet of God and could not have such a servant mucking up the works. Gehazi's punishment was well deserved. *For the full story of Elisha's greedy servant, read 2 Kings 5:1–27.*

# Good News, Bad News

*Jehu Has News for King Jehoshaphat*

Factoids: Jehoshaphat
- *Domicile:* Jerusalem
- *Date:* Around 870–850 B.C.
- *Occupation:* King of the southern kingdom of Judah
- *Family Ties:* Father, Asa; mother, Azubah; son, Jehoram; daughter-in-law, Athaliah
- *Mentioned in the Bible:* 1 Kings 15:24; 22:1–50; 2 Kings 3:1–14; 2 Chronicles 17:1–21:1; Joel 3:2, 12

"I HAVE GOOD NEWS and bad news. Which do you want first?" Sometimes people ask for the good news because they can't wait for it. More often, people want the bad news first, because then, once they hear the good news, the bad news doesn't seem so bad.

That's the theory anyway. But bad news is still bad news.

The prophet Jehu (there's also a king named Jehu, so don't get confused) had a message for King Jehoshaphat. The message occupies only two verses in the Bible, but he manages to give the king both bad news and good news—with the bad news coming first.

"Why should you help the wicked and love those who late the LORD?" Jehu asked. "Because of what you have done, the LORD is very angry with you" (2 Chronicles 19:2 NLT). Not exactly the kind of news a king wants right after barely escaping with his life from the battlefield.

To understand exactly what Jehoshaphat had done that so angered the Lord, we have to go back a couple of chapters in 2 Chronicles. The trouble started at the beginning of chapter 18. Jehoshaphat had tried to be a good king. Up in the northern kingdom of Israel, Ahab was king—a very wicked man, whose wife, Jezebel, had brought Baal worship into the kingdom. For some completely unknown reason, Jehoshaphat decided that he needed to make an alliance with the northern kingdom, and did so by having his son marry Ahab and Jezebel's daughter.

So now they were all one big, happy family—sort of.

Then Ahab decided that he wanted to attack Ramoth-gilead, and asked Jehoshaphat to join him. Jehoshaphat replied, "Why, of course! You and I are as one, and my troops are your troops. We will certainly join you in battle." Then he added, almost as an afterthought, "But first let's find out what the LORD says" (18:3–4).

(Good idea, O king who is supposed to be following the Lord.)

Prophets did go and talk to Ahab and Jehoshaphat—that story is told in "The Bearer of Bad News" (page 129). Even though God's prophet, Micaiah, had told the kings *not* to attack Ramoth-gilead, they went anyway. True to Micaiah's words, Ahab was killed, and Jehoshaphat was saved only by the Lord's intervention.

So Jehoshaphat returned home, only to be met by the condemnation of Jehu and the Lord. Before the battle, Jehoshaphat had wanted to hear what God's prophet would say; God's prophet had spoken, but Jehoshaphat ignored the warning and went against God's word. No wonder the Lord was angry.

But Jehu also had good news. "Even so, there is some good in you, for you have removed the Asherah poles throughout the land, and you have committed yourself to seeking God" (2 Chronicles 19:3).

God saw the good in Jehoshaphat, even as he had to intervene and save the king's hide on the battlefield.

Jehoshaphat's life was good at times and bad at times. In the end, however, "He did what was pleasing in the LORD's sight" (20:32).

Now that's good news.

*Read Jehu's snappy words for Jehoshaphat in 2 Chronicles 19:1–3.*

# Ready to Go

*Isaiah Sees an Unexpected Sight—God*

Factoids: Isaiah
- *Domicile:* Jerusalem
- *Date:* Around 740 B.C.
- *Occupation:* Scribe, prophet
- *Family Ties:* Father, Amoz; sons, Shear-Jashub and Maher-Shalal-Hash-Baz.
- *Mentioned or quoted in the Bible:* 2 Kings 19:2–20:19; 2 Chronicles 26:22; 32:20, 32; book of Isaiah; Matthew 1:22–23, 3:3, 4:14–16; 8:17; 12:17–21; 13:14; 15:7; Mark 1:2; 7:6; Luke 3:4; 4:17–19; John 1:23; 12:38–41; Romans 10:16, 20–21

MOST OF US have a basic belief that while we make mistakes, we're still fairly "good" people. But Isaiah, whom many would have called a good man, was confronted by the proof of his sin. All it took was for him to see God.

That's right. *See* God—something not too many people could claim and live to tell about it.

Isaiah had a respectable occupation as a palace scribe, but the year King Uzziah of Judah died he experienced a career change. The catalyst was an amazing vision of God seated on a throne above which were seraphs (six-winged angels). This vision of God's holiness and splendor was duplicated only by John's vision in the book of Revelation.

Well, such a sight inspired great fear in Isaiah, as he instantly recognized his sinfulness. "Woe to me! I am ruined! For I am a man of unclean lips, and I live among a people of unclean lips, and my eyes have seen the King, the LORD Almighty" (Isaiah 6:5 NIV). He was expecting an instantaneous end to his life.

But one of the angels took a live coal from the altar and touched his lips, declaring Isaiah clean before God.

Then Isaiah heard the voice of the Lord asking who would be willing to go and declare God's words to the people. His response? "Here am I. Send me!" (6:8).

Sometimes we get swept up in the moment, overwhelmed by the powerful urge to reach out to others, to evangelize, to minister to those in need. This must have been one of those moments for Isaiah.

God told Isaiah the people would listen to his messages but not learn from them. Their hearts had become cold. But Isaiah was still to speak God's messages. Although the nation of Judah as a whole would not return to God, some individuals *would* listen.

After this vision of God on the throne, Isaiah went on to prophesy about the coming King of kings, who would come to earth as a man to suffer and die on behalf of all. This man—Immanuel—would ultimately make any who trusted in him clean before God, without having to use a coal to do so. He would be Jesus, the Savior who would later quote from the prophet Isaiah more than any other prophet.

All because Isaiah was ready and willing to go.

*To read about Isaiah's call to a complete career change, see Isaiah 6. See also Isaiah 7 and 53.*

# A True Book Burning

*Jeremiah's Scroll Is Destroyed by the King*

Factoids: Jeremiah
- *Domicile:* Anathoth, a village in the southern kingdom of Judah
- *Date:* Probably ministered between 627 and 586 B.C.
- *Occupation:* Prophet
- *Family Ties:* Father, Hilkiah
- *Mentioned in the Bible:* Ezra 1:1; book of Jeremiah; Daniel 9:2; Matthew 2:17; 16:14; 27:9

B OOK BURNING has often been a sign of protest across the ages. The first emperor of China, Qin Shi Huang, unified China in the year 221 B.C. One goal was to unify thoughts and opinions by way of controlling what people could read. In a move that causes today's historians to shudder, hundreds of classic works were burned—

everything except those written by the emperor's own historians. Any local authorities who did not burn the listed books within thirty days were forced to end their careers and become slaves working on the Great Wall.

Usually motivated by some kind of political or moral uprising, burning books in a great bonfire in the center of town certainly makes a statement. And that's the kind of statement that King Jehoiakim wanted to make.

The southern kingdom of Judah was in a downward spiral. Jehoiakim's father, Josiah, had been a good king in his early days, but in the latter part of his reign had turned away from God; he was killed by Pharaoh Neco in a battle against Egypt. His son Jehoahaz was made king, but only for three months. Pharaoh Neco came into Judah, imposed a heavy tax on the people, took Jehoahaz away in chains, and "made Eliakim son of Josiah king in place of his father Josiah and changed Eliakim's name to Jehoiakim" (2 Kings 23:34 NIV). The Bible says that "he did evil in the eyes of the LORD, just as his fathers did" (23:37). Jehoiakim was really no more than a puppet ruler. During his reign, Nebuchadnezzar, king of Babylon, invaded and took many people back to Babylon (this was when Daniel and his friends were deported), and Jehoiakim had a new guy pulling his strings.

In the fourth year of Jehoiakim's reign, God told Jeremiah, "Take a scroll and write on it all the words I have spoken to you concerning Israel, Judah and all the other nations from the time I began speaking to you in the reign of Josiah till now" (Jeremiah 36:2). That was a lot of messages! So Jeremiah called his trusty scribe Baruch and dictated all his messages.

After he wrote it all down, Jeremiah sent Baruch to read the scroll in the temple to all the people who visited there. Jeremiah himself had been restricted from entering the temple because of his rantings—but that didn't stop God. With the words of the prophet written on the scroll, Baruch dutifully read the prophecies to the people.

And they were terrified. Then a royal official got wind of what was occurring, so he sent for Baruch and had the scroll read at a special meeting. When he finished, the officials in the meeting "looked at each other in fear" (36:16).

What was the message that was so terrifying? Oh, little things like:

> Therefore the LORD Almighty says this: "Because you have not listened to my words, I will summon all the peoples of the north and my servant Nebuchadnezzar king of Babylon," declares the LORD, "and I will bring them against this land and its inhabitants and against all the surrounding nations. I will completely destroy them and make them an object of horror and scorn, and an everlasting ruin. I will banish from them the sounds of joy and gladness, the voices of bride and bridegroom, the sound of millstones and the light of the lamp. This whole country will become a desolate wasteland, and these nations will serve the king of Babylon seventy years." (Jeremiah 25:8–11)

No wonder Jeremiah had gotten himself into so much trouble! Words like this sounded treasonous. But the prophecy also offered hope: all the people needed to do was turn back to God.

The officials decided that King Jehoiakim needed to hear the message. The scroll was taken to Jehudi, who then read it to the king, who was sitting beside a fire, warming himself in the chilly winter air.

And Jehoiakim did a book burning. "Whenever Jehudi had read three or four columns of the scroll, the king cut them off with a scribe's knife and threw them into the firepot, until the entire scroll was burned in the fire" (36:23).

Jehoiakim thought that burning the scroll would show his protest against these dire prophecies, that he didn't care, that he didn't believe in all this nonsense.

But God's message came again to Jeremiah: "Tell Baruch to sharpen his pencil. We're gonna do it again!"

And the message came true, of course, in every point. Burning the scroll didn't change the truth of God's words.

*To find out more about Jeremiah's message and the king's book burning, read Jeremiah 36.*

# A Tough Task

*Ezekiel Is Told to Speak, Even Though No One Will Listen*

Factoids: Ezekiel
- *Domicile:* Babylon
- *Date:* Probably ministered around 595 B.C.
- *Occupation:* Prophet
- *Family Ties:* Father, Buzi; wife, unnamed
- *Mentioned in the Bible:* 2 Kings 24:10–17 the book of Ezekiel

CATCH-22 IS A PHRASE coined by writer Joseph Heller, referring to a situation in which a person will lose, no matter what choice he or she makes. When God called the prophet Ezekiel to action, Ezekiel's task was to speak to a people who would not listen or would be extremely angry with him. But if he said no to the job, he would be in trouble with God. A catch-22, all right.

Ezekiel was called to be God's spokesman 150 years after Isaiah, during Israel's captivity in Babylon. The day probably began like any other day. But then something extraordinary happened: Ezekiel saw "visions of God" (Ezekiel 1:1 NIV). It began with a windstorm, flashing lightning, and fire. But with that came four creatures, each of which had four faces and four wings. These were cherubim, he later discovered. These were not the Hallmark/Valentine's Day kind of cherubim. While they had a roughly humanoid shape, they had the faces of a man, an ox, a lion, and an eagle. What was more, they glowed with the fire passed between them.

Near each cherub was a wheel crossed in the center by another wheel—"a wheel in the middle of a wheel" (1:16 KJV). These wheels had eyes all over them. The cherubim manipulated the wheels. This was a symbol of God's ability to see and control the events on the earth.

Above the cherubim, Ezekiel saw a throne upon which sat the figure of a man—a man who "looked like glowing metal, as if full of fire" (1:27 NIV).

Like Isaiah, who also saw a vision of God in his temple (see "Ready to Go," page 135), Ezekiel was stunned nearly senseless. But God began to speak, introducing the task he had for Ezekiel. He began with a familiar description of Israel: "The people to whom I am sending you are obstinate and stubborn" (2:4). Their propensity to sin and not repent, decade after decade, century after century, was the reason behind their exile in Babylon. Yet God loved them enough to continue to send them prophets.

Whereas Isaiah prophesied about the coming captivity if Israel refused to repent, Ezekiel was given the difficult task of prophesying to those in the midst of the captivity. As a result of their circumstances, the people were ungrateful and prone to mistreat the prophets of God. But the Lord told Ezekiel, "Do not be afraid of them or their words. Do not be afraid though briers and thorns are all around you and you live among scorpions. Do not be afraid of what they say or terrified by them" (2:6–7). After the third time of hearing "Do not be afraid," surely Ezekiel must have wondered what he was getting himself into.

But God gave Ezekiel a small ray of hope by telling him that "whether they listen or fail to listen . . . they will know that a prophet has been among them" (2:5). God's Spirit was now with Ezekiel and there would be no mistaking who sent him. It was a tough task, but Ezekiel was going to do it.

*To read about Ezekiel's strange and wonderful vision and call to ministry, read Ezekiel 1–2.*

# Talk to the Hand

*Daniel Interprets What the Hand Writes*

Factoids: Daniel
- *Domicile:* From Judah, taken captive by the Babylonians
- *Date:* Probably ministered between 586 and 536 B.C.
- *Occupation:* High government official and adviser for Babylonian kings, and later for Medo-Persian kings
- *Family Ties:* None named; contemporaries were Shadrach, Meshach, Abednego, Nebuchadnezzar, Belshazzar, Darius, and Cyrus
- *Mentioned in the Bible:* The book of Daniel; Matthew 24:15

SOME PEOPLE just know how to ruin a good party. In this case, it was just part of a person that ruined a party—specifically, a hand.

Belshazzar was serving as coregent of the Babylonian empire along with his father, Nabonidus, who came to power in a line of kings following the great Nebuchadnezzar.

Belshazzar wanted to have a party, so he invited thousands of nobles to a great banquet. As the wine flowed, Belshazzar had what he thought was a stunningly brilliant idea (too much wine can sometimes make people think stupid things are brilliant). He called for the gold and silver goblets that his predecessor Nebuchadnezzar had plundered from the temple in Jerusalem.

On that fateful day when Nebuchadnezzar's army invaded the city, "they took away the pots and the shovels and the snuffers and the dishes for incense and all the vessels of bronze used in the temple service, the fire pans also and the bowls. What was of gold the captain of the guard took away as gold, and what was of silver, as silver" (2 Kings 25:14–15 ESV).

So apparently these goblets had been stored somewhere in the palace, and Belshazzar thought it would be a great idea to bring out these sacred items (sacred to the Jews) and use them for serving wine to his guests. So the goblets were brought out and filled with wine. Then, as the king and nobles and wives and concubines drank, they "praised the gods of gold and silver, bronze, iron, wood, and stone" (Daniel 5:4). That was the second not-so-brilliant idea.

And that's when the party went south, quickly. Suddenly, all the guests saw a human hand appear against the plaster wall of the banquet hall. And . . . it was writing some words. Probably a few of the guests put down their golden goblets, thinking they had had *way* too much to drink. But what they were seeing was real. Problem was, no one could read the words that the hand was writing on the wall. The terrified king brought in all the wise men and astrologers and magicians, offering a big reward to whoever could interpret the writing. But no one could do it.

Then the queen (probably Nabonidus's wife) remembered Daniel, now an elderly man who had served Nebuchadnezzar. She knew the story of how he had interpreted dreams and answered all kinds of difficult problems. "Let Daniel be called," she said.

And so he was. Daniel came in, and Belshazzar gave him the same spiel about getting all kinds of rewards and even being honored as third ruler in the kingdom.

Daniel might have chuckled if the situation weren't so serious. *Yeah, right,* he might have thought, *third ruler of the Babylonian empire for all of about thirty minutes.* The words on the wall spoke of the coming destruction of the Babylonian empire, starting right there in Babylon . . . that very night.

And so it happened. Darius and the combined forces of the Medes and Persians overthrew Babylon and took over as the next world empire.

Party poopers, indeed.

*Read about the scary hand and Belshazzar's ruined party in Daniel 5.*

## PROPHETS IN THE BIBLE

| Prophet | Date | Writings or Referred to in Scripture |
|---------|------|--------------------------------------|
| Moses | Unknown | Exodus through Deuteronomy |
| Miriam | Unknown | Exodus 2; 15; Numbers 12 |
| Deborah | Unknown | Judges 4–5 |
| Samuel | Unknown | 1 Samuel 1–28 |
| Nathan | 1010–970 B.C. | 2 Samuel 7–1 Kings 1 |
| Gad | Around 950 B.C. | 2 Samuel 24:11–14 |
| Ahijah | 943–909 B.C. | 1 Kings 11:29–39 |
| Elijah | 875–848 B.C. | 1 Kings 17:1–2 Kings 2:11 |
| Micaiah | 865–853 B.C. | 1 Kings 22:8–38; 2 Chronicles 18 |
| Obadiah | 855–840 B.C. | Book of Obadiah |
| Jehu | 853 B.C. | 2 Chronicles 19:1–3 |

| PROPHET | DATE | WRITINGS OR REFERRED TO IN SCRIPTURE |
|---------|------|--------------------------------------|
| Elisha | 848–797 B.C. | 1 Kings 19:16–2 Kings 13:20 |
| Joel | 835–796 B.C. | Book of Joel |
| Jonah | 793–753 B.C. | 2 Kings 14:25; book of Jonah |
| Amos | 760–750 B.C. | Book of Amos |
| Hosea | 753–715 B.C. | Book of Hosea |
| Micah | 742–687 B.C. | Book of Micah |
| Isaiah | 740–681 B.C. | 2 Kings 19–20; 2 Chronicles 26; 32; the book of Isaiah |
| Zephaniah | 640–621 B.C. | Book of Zephaniah |
| Huldah | 632 B.C. | 2 Kings 22:14–20 |
| Jeremiah | 627–586 B.C. | Book of Jeremiah |
| Habakkuk | 612–589 B.C. | Book of Habakkuk |
| Daniel | 605–536 B.C. | Book of Daniel |
| Ezekiel | 593–571 B.C. | Book of Ezekiel |
| Haggai | 530 B.C. | Book of Haggai |
| Zechariah | 520 B.C. | Book of Zechariah |
| Malachi | 430 B.C. | Book of Malachi |
| John the Baptist | A.D. 30 | Malachi 4:5–6; Matthew 3:1–17; 17:10–12; Mark 1:1–8; Luke 3:1–18 |
| Agabus | A.D. 59 | Acts 11:28; 21:10–11 |
| Philip's daughters | A.D. 59 | Acts 21:9 |

# Weird Wedding

*Hosea Marries a Prostitute Named Gomer*

SOME PEOPLE SAY the Bible is boring. Apparently, they never read as far as the Song of Songs, or the book of Daniel, or this little book by a prophet named Hosea. People go to the tabloids for sex, adventure, and jaw-dropping stories—little do most people know they can find all that right in the pages of the Bible.

Hosea was called to speak to his own people, the wayward Israelites living in the northern kingdom. While the southern kingdom of Judah had a few God-fearing kings who brought the nation back to God at intermittent points, the northern kingdom of Israel had not one good king. All of them were evil, leading the people away from God and into idolatry. The nation was fairly prosperous, so apparently the people didn't think they needed God. Hosea was called to bring God's word during the reigns of its last six kings and up until the time of their annihilation at the hands of the Assyrians.

God's message was simple: The nation had been unfaithful to the God who loved them, "committing adultery" by their worship of other gods.

And God gave the people this message in living color.

He told Hosea, "Israel has betrayed me like an unfaithful wife. Marry such a woman and have children by her" (Hosea 1:2 CEV).

Whoa! Imagine getting *that* message with your coffee on a Monday morning!

God wanted to make a point. The lives of the prophets were watched carefully by the people—they wanted to hear messages from the Lord, although they usually rejected the message if they didn't like it. So consider their surprise as they watched the prophet take a prostitute off the street and into the wedding chapel (so to speak). If it had been Las Vegas, maybe no one would have looked twice. But this was the local prophet, and it was *weird*.

Hosea did have children with Gomer, and he couldn't even be sure if they were his. Then, at one point, despite Hosea's tender care for Gomer, she ran off with another man.

So God sent another difficult task to Hosea: "Go, show your love to your wife again, though she is loved by another and is an adulteress. Love her as the LORD loves the Israelites, though they turn to other gods and love the sacred raisin cakes" (Hosea 3:1 NIV).

So Hosea went and brought her back, loved her, and cared for her.

The message? God loves his people—all his people—and even when they mess up and sin, he wants them back. And he'll do whatever it takes.

The Bible, boring? No way!

*Read about Hosea's stormy relationship with Gomer in Hosea 1–3.*

# Facing the Swarm

*Joel Prophesies About the Coming of Locusts*

WHEN JOEL GAVE his prophecy of a coming swarm of locusts, his listeners understood the danger. And several millennia later, locust plagues still affect the world. How terrible is the devastation? In a January 7, 2005, article on nationalgeographic .com/news appears the following description:

> During massive plagues, desert locusts can appear over a land area of nearly 12 million square miles (30 million square kilometers) in some 60 nations—comprising over 20 percent of Earth's land surface. The insects inflict heavy crop damage that's devastating for subsistence farmers, many of whom must flee land that can no longer support their families. The FAO's [the United Nation's Food and Agriculture Organization] Desert Locust Information Service reports that during the biggest plagues, the insects may endanger the livelihood of one in every ten people on Earth.

Clearly, these little insects are still a force to be reckoned with.

Listen as Joel described an invasion of locusts across the land: They are without number (Joel 1:6); they destroy everything in their path (1:10–12); they plunge forward like an army, not swerving or fluttering, but almost with purpose (2:7–8); they fill homes (2:9); and their numbers are so huge that they darken the sky (2:10).

The same online article continues to say that these plagues cannot be predicted any better than we can predict the weather.

But God knows.

Locusts had descended on Egypt at Moses's command as one of the ten plagues God visited on that nation (Exodus 10:1–20). In the book of Joel, God may have already sent a plague upon his people, which Joel described here, or Joel may have been using this symbolic description of locust devastation to describe something far worse that was coming.

Joel prophesied to the southern kingdom of Judah around 835 to 796 B.C. The nation was experiencing ups and downs with the overthrow of a wicked queen (Athaliah) and the crowning of a seven-year-old king (Joash), who followed God for a while and then turned away. God was going to punish his people for their sinfulness. Joel correctly prophesied the coming of a nation that would, like a plague of locusts, completely decimate them. That nation was Babylon, and Joel's description came true in 586 B.C., when a final invasion by the Babylonians brought Judah to its knees. The Babylonians laid siege to Jerusalem, and "the famine in the city had become so severe that there was no food for the people to eat. Then the city wall was broken through, and the whole army fled at night" (2 Kings 25:3–4 NIV). God's temple was dismantled and burned, and the people were either killed or taken into captivity.

Joel's prophecy came true to the smallest detail.

But Joel saw more than just destruction. He saw a glorious future for God's people, a day of restoration. In fact, buried in the middle of his little book are words that the apostle Peter quoted on the day of Pentecost: "I will pour out my Spirit on all people. Your sons and daughters will prophesy, your old men will dream dreams, your young men will see visions" (Joel 2:28). Centuries later, more of Joel's prophecy came true the day the Holy Spirit came upon the Christians gathered in Jerusalem, shortly after Jesus' return to heaven. (Read about it in Acts 2.)

And what about the prophecies of the future return of Christ and an eternity with him for all who believe? Well, we can count on the truth of those prophecies, too, because we can trust the God who gave them. Locust plagues may be unpredictable, but God's Word is never in doubt.

*Read all about the hungry army of locusts in Joel 2.*

# Amos, the Assyrians, and Almighty God

## *Amos Speaks God's Message Against Social Injustice*

GOD CALLS PEOPLE from all walks of life. Amos was minding his own business, watching his sheep in the village of Tekoa, when the Lord called him. A peace-loving shepherd was called to announce some pretty harsh judgments.

Amos was from the southern kingdom of Judah, but his message was directed at the northern kingdom of Israel. Amos prophesied about God's coming punishment for various surrounding kingdoms that had caused great suffering to God's people. He spoke against Aram (Syria), Philistia, Tyre, Edom, Ammon, and Moab. Next, Amos leveled his message against his own people to the south, the southern kingdom of Judah.

Such messages were a welcome relief to the northern kingdom.

They were home free, right? Wrong. Another message hit home, literally, when Amos pointed his finger directly at the people of the northern kingdom and prophesied their destruction.

The people may have listened intently to Amos's prophecies against the nations around them, but probably scoffed at the words spoken against them. After all, the nation of Israel was affluent, enjoying peace and prosperity. What could possibly be wrong?

"I'll tell you what's wrong," and Amos proceeded to enumerate the people's sins, not the least of which was rampant social injustice: The people had become materialistic; the wealthy ignored the needs of the poor; they had become self-centered; they ignored their God.

Amos used a series of word pictures as he gave his message: Like a loaded cart that collapses under the weight of too much grain, so the nation would collapse under its own affluence (Amos 2:13). Like the terrifying roar of a lion, the Lord had spoken and his word is always true (3:8). Amos described a scene he may have observed in the fields with the flocks—the bones of a mutilated sheep taken by a lion—to explain that the destruction of the nation would be complete, although a few people would be saved (3:12). Amos pictured the arrogance of the wealthy women who oppressed the poor and needy as though they were pampered cows on the hills of Samaria (4:1-3). Amos saw the vision of a plumb line, and God showed him just how far "off" the people had gone (7:7-8). Like a basket of ripe fruit, the nation's sin had caused it to be ripe for punishment (8:1-2).

The people did not repent at Amos's words, and God did bring the judgment he promised—courtesy of the Assyrian army.

It just doesn't pay to mess with Almighty God.

*Read all the gory details of these prophetic judgments in Amos 1–9.*

# Over and Out

*Obadiah Sees a Vision About the Country of Edom*

THE PROPHET OBADIAH has the distinction of having written the shortest book in the Bible. You'll find his prophecy buried in the section called "Minor Prophets" (Hosea through Malachi), at the end of the Old Testament. The term *minor* only means that their books are short. They still played major roles as God's spokesmen.

Obadiah was a prophet to the southern kingdom of Judah. While we don't know much about him or even exactly when he lived and prophesied, we do know that God gave him an important message, and that his message was fulfilled in every detail.

To understand Obadiah's prophecy, we need to travel in time, back to the book of Genesis and the story of Isaac and Rebekah's twin sons, Jacob and Esau. Even when these boys were in utero they were at each other's throats. Rebekah was so disturbed by the constant kicking and jostling in her womb that she asked God about it. And God gave a startling answer: "Two nations are in your womb, and two peoples from within you will be separated; one people will be stronger than the other, and the older will serve the younger" (Genesis 25:23 NIV).

Esau was older than Jacob by a few minutes, and the Bible even tells us that Jacob had hold of Esau's foot when they were born (25:26). The story of how Jacob received both the birthright and the blessing, even though he was the younger son, is told in Genesis 25–27. There was no love lost between these two brothers. Even though they eventually made peace with each other, the nations that descended from them were constantly at odds.

Esau's descendants became the Edomites, who settled in the region southeast of the Dead Sea. Jacob's descendants became the nation of Israel, the Hebrews.

It wasn't long before age-old animosity reared its ugly head. As the Hebrew people made their way toward the Promised Land after having wandered for forty years, they needed to travel north from the desert, through the country of Edom. Moses sent messengers to the king of Edom asking permission to pass through the land: "This is what your brother Israel says . . . Please let us pass through your country. We will not go through any field or vineyard, or drink water from any well. We will travel along the king's highway and not turn to the right or to the left until we have passed through your territory" (Numbers 20:14, 17).

The response? "Edom answered: 'You may not pass through here; if you try, we will march out and attack you with the sword.' . . . Then Edom came out against them with a large and powerful army. Since Edom refused to let them go through their territory, Israel turned away from them" (20:18, 20–21).

As time passed and foreign empires subjugated the northern and southern kingdoms of Israel and Judah as well as Edom, the Edomites gloated whenever their Hebrew neighbors faced misfortune. "Any enemy of theirs is a friend of ours" seems to have been their motto.

So God sent Obadiah to explain just what the future held for these people. They had "stood aloof" while Jerusalem was being plundered; they had even marched through the gates along with the enemy to take plunder for themselves. When anyone tried to escape the invaders, the Edomites would wait along escape routes to capture and kill them or turn them over to the enemy (Obadiah 11–14).

Brotherly love at its finest.

But God would have the final say. As they had treated their brothers, that's how they would be treated. Obadiah prophesied that "there will be no survivors from the house of Esau" (Obadiah 18). Around 164 B.C., Judas Maccabeus routed the Edomites and the nation ceased to exist.

Try to find it on a map today. You can't. It's gone. Such is the fate of those who defy God.

*Read Obadiah's big prophecy in his little book in the Old Testament.*

# A Fish Tale

*Jonah Avoids Going to Nineveh and Finds a Fish Instead*

Factoids: Jonah
- *Domicile*: Likely from Gath Hepher (since that was where his father was from)
- *Family Ties*: Father, Amittai the prophet
- *Occupation:* Prophet
- *Mentioned in the Bible:* Kings 14:25; the book of Jonah

MANY MIGHT THINK of the story of Jonah as having elements of Herman Melville's classic story, *Moby-Dick*—a tale of an angry man's search for the elusive white whale who was the bane of his existence. But instead of searching for the "great fish," as it is called in the Bible (Jonah 1:17 NIV), Jonah was *found* by one. All because he thought he could run from God.

Jonah was called by God to preach to the nation of Assyria, the capital of which was Nineveh. But Jonah wanted nothing to do with sharing God's word with the people who had treated the Israelites cruelly. So, instead of heading east, he hopped on a ship and sailed west.

When a raging storm threatened everyone on board the ship, the pagan sailors had to remind Jonah—who was fast asleep belowdecks—to seek the help of his God. His conscience didn't even bother him enough to keep him from getting a good rest!

When the sailors cast lots and found out Jonah was somehow responsible for the storm, he told them he was running from the Lord. Jonah knew the solution to the problem: "Pick me up and throw me into the sea, and it will become calm. I know this is my fault that this great storm has come upon you" (1:12).

Reluctantly, the mariners threw him overboard, and the sea instantly became calm. But Jonah didn't drown. Instead a huge fish swallowed him.

It's hard to imagine a marine animal large enough to swallow a man whole and keep him intact for three days and nights. This, however, was a special fish, created by God for the purpose of rescuing and transporting Jonah.

While in the belly of the fish, Jonah cried out to God. His prayer continued as a prayer of thanksgiving—that he was still breathing; that God had rescued him, even in this unusual way.

When Jonah found himself in the sunlight on the beach, we can be certain that he praised the Lord again. And this time when God told him to go to Nineveh, he went without hesitation.

Jonah completed his mission and his fear of the people of Ninevah's not getting punished for their actions was confirmed: the people actually repented and God vowed to spare them from destruction. Although Jonah's reaction to the news did not reflect God's love (read about that in "An Unjust Jonah," page 30), his story illustrates the far-reaching mercy of God, a mercy he extends to disobedient people and pouting prophets alike.

*To read about Jonah and his deep-sea encounter, read Jonah 1–3.*

# Big News
# for Bethlehem

*Micah Prophesies the Birthplace of the Messiah*

THE PROMISE OF A SAVIOR had been a ray of hope for the Hebrew people for centuries. Many of the prophets spoke of a coming Messiah, a Savior, who would bring justice, restoration, and salvation. Some spoke of his death, others spoke of his miracles and teachings, still others of his demeanor.

And Micah, the prophet from Moresheth, a little village in the southern kingdom of Judah, gave the location of his birth.

Micah also spoke about other things. He spoke about judgment against the nation because of their great sinfulness. Rampant greed, debauchery, injustice, and oppression were taking the nation down a slippery slope to destruction.

But even in the most dire of prophecies, God always gave a ray of hope. In Micah's case, it promised a future ruler who would be born in Bethlehem: "But you, O Bethlehem Ephrathah, who are too little to be among the clans of Judah, from you shall come forth for me one who is to be ruler in Israel, whose origin is from of old, from ancient days" (Micah 5:2 ESV).

In fact, centuries later, when the wise men arrived in the nation of Judea after having followed the star, they asked of King Herod, "Where is he who has been born king of the Jews? For we saw his star when it rose and have come to worship him" (Matthew 2:2).

King Herod, disturbed by the news, sent for the Jewish scribes and chief priests, asking them where this new king was to be born. They opened their scrolls and pointed directly to Micah's prophecy, rightly identifying for Herod the location of Jesus' birth. When the wise men made their way to the tiny village, they found the newborn king.

So ingrained was this knowledge of the Messiah's birthplace that, ironically, it became a source of contention during Jesus' ministry. Jesus had indeed been born in Bethlehem, but when he was very young, his parents had settled in Nazareth (in the region of Galilee) and there he had grown up.

Once when Jesus was on the verge of being arrested by the religious leaders, he had spoken so eloquently that many who heard him thought he was the Christ. But others asked, "Has not the Scripture said that the Christ comes from the offspring of David, and comes from Bethlehem, the village where David was?" (John 7:42). The people were divided over his identity because of his birthplace. If these questioners had just taken the time to find out the facts, they wouldn't have been so confused!

The prophets knew. The people should have known. Where are you on the question of who Jesus is?

*Micah's far-reaching prophecy about Jesus' birthplace is in Micah 5:2.*

# Nahum and Nineveh

*Nahum Prophesies About God's Judgment on the Capital of the Assyrian Empire*

THE PROPHETS Nahum and Jonah might have shared notes, for both men were called by God to bring a message against the great city of Nineveh.

While we learn a lot about Jonah and his simple message in his book (see "A Fish Tale," page 154), we know virtually nothing about Nahum. They are separated by a century. Perhaps when Nahum was called to bring the message of destruction to Nineveh, he knew, based on Jonah's experience, that he'd better do as God said.

Jonah brought a call to repentance, and, astoundingly, the city responded and repented. Now, one hundred years later, the city was as evil as ever and its days were numbered.

The city of Nineveh boasted a wall that stretched for eight miles, enclosing a city of about 1,700 acres. When Jonah had visited the city, the population had been "more than a hundred and twenty thousand people" (Jonah 4:11 NIV). The city was the capital of the mighty Assyrian empire, which dominated the region from 900 B.C. to around 600 B.C. The Assyrian army was renowned for its cruelty. When Nahum was called to prophesy, the nation had already destroyed the northern kingdom of Israel and slaughtered the people or taken them into captivity. The southern kingdom of Judah was still subject to Assyria and experienced great suffering because of it.

But God was watching. The city was ripe for his punishment, and so Nahum brought words of final judgment: "Nothing can heal your wound; your injury is fatal. Everyone who hears the news about you claps his hands at your fall, for who has not felt your endless cruelty?" (Nahum 3:19).

Bet Jonah wishes he'd gotten to bring *that* message to Nineveh.

Nahum's fellow prophet, Zephaniah, gave a description of the coming desolation:

> [God] will stretch out his hand against the north and destroy Assyria, leaving Nineveh utterly desolate and dry as the desert. Flocks and herds will lie down there, creatures of every kind. The desert owl and the screech owl will roost on her columns. Their calls will echo through the windows, rubble will be in the doorways, the beams of cedar will be exposed. This is the carefree city that lived in safety. She said to herself, "I am, and there is none besides me." What a ruin she has become, a lair for wild beasts! All who pass by her scoff and shake their fists. (Zephaniah 2:13–15)

True to God's words through his prophets, Nineveh was overthrown in 612 B.C. by the Babylonians, who became the new world power. The destruction was so complete that it was never rebuilt. For centuries it lay covered with the desert sands. Only recently have archaeologists begun to discover the treasures of Nineveh— a great, arrogant, and cruel city brought down by God.

*For more on Nahum's tough words for Nineveh, read Nahum 1–3.*

# A Heavenly Q&A

*Habakkuk Complains to God*

WHEN YOU HAVE A QUESTION about a pain in your side, you go to a doctor. When you have a concern about why your dishwasher is leaking, you call a plumber. When you have a toothache, you go to the dentist.

Obvious, right?

But when people have questions about life, the world, good and evil, and the future, many folks take these questions to all the wrong places. They look at their horoscopes in the local paper, or they visit a palm reader to read them the tarot cards. They may simply decide for themselves, based on reading authors from previous generations, that this life is a hopeless exercise in futility, so they should live to please themselves—after all, "one shot is all you got."

Habakkuk was a prophet to the southern kingdom of Judah, sometime between 612 and 588 B.C. The northern kingdom of Israel had already ceased to exist, having been destroyed by the Assyrians in 722 B.C., and then the Assyrian capital at Nineveh had fallen in 612 B.C. A new empire was gaining power—the Babylonians—and the tiny nation of Judah watched and wondered what was coming next. Clearly, much was going on in Habakkuk's world—worthy of a twenty-four-hour news channel.

Habakkuk watched the growth of this new empire with concern. He also looked around and saw the evil in his own land. The final four kings of the southern kingdom were all evil men who rejected God. It wouldn't be long before the Babylonians found their way to Judah. And in fact, Judah was invaded twice, before a final invasion in 586 B.C. that destroyed it.

With all his heart Habakkuk longed for change. He wanted his people to wake up and smell the coming destruction! But the nation continued to spiral downward even as the Babylonians became the next dominant world power.

So, like any good prophet, Habakkuk took his questions to God. He asked why God was not punishing the evil leaders in his own land who were leading the people astray. "How long, O LORD, must I call for help, but you do not listen? Or cry out to you, 'Violence!' but you do not save?" (Habakkuk 1:2 NIV).

God's answer was, in essence, "Don't worry, Habakkuk. They'll get theirs. In fact, I have a special surprise for my sinful and rebellious people." The surprise? "I am raising up the Babylonians, that ruthless and impetuous people, who sweep across the whole earth to seize dwelling places not their own" (1:6).

Now wait a minute! The Babylonians? Aren't they just as bad? God just described them as "ruthless and impetuous"! Why would he use bad people to punish bad people? That doesn't make any sense. Judah may have been bad, but they were way better than Babylon! "Why are you silent while the wicked swallow up those more righteous than themselves?" Habakkuk wondered (1:13). To him, God's plan was a little goofy, to say the least.

So Habakkuk got himself some flatbread chips and a grape soda, climbed up to the ramparts of the city, and waited for God's answer.

Habakkuk was not disappointed. God did answer. God explained that although the evil nation of Babylon would be used to punish the evil nation of Judah, eventually Babylon would be punished as well. (You can read that story in "Talk to the Hand," page 142). "Write this down," God told Habakkuk. "Future peoples will need to understand that I've got it all under control." Nothing happens on this entire planet without God's hand in it. Nations rise and fall due to God's overarching plan.

"When will justice come?" we might ask with Habakkuk. God

answered that too: "For the revelation awaits an appointed time; it speaks of the end and will not prove false. Though it linger, wait for it; it will certainly come and will not delay" (2:3).

In other words, be patient. God says that he will make everything right one day. And in the end, "The righteous will live by his faith" (2:4).

Evil is a reality in our world, but we must never lose hope that God is in control. The New Testament writers quoted Habakkuk as they brought the message of faith and hope. As Paul explained the power of the gospel message to the Romans, he wrote, "For in the gospel a righteousness from God is revealed, a righteousness that is by faith from first to last, just as it is written: 'The righteous will live by faith'" (Romans 1:17). To the believers in Galatia who were struggling to live faithful lives, Paul wrote, "Clearly no one is justified before God by the law, because, 'The righteous will live by faith'" (Galatians 3:11).

The writer of the book of Hebrews offered hope to those who suffered persecution for their faith. The readers may have been asking the same questions Habakkuk had: Why was God allowing an evil nation (in their case, the Roman empire) to flourish and to persecute God's people, the Christians? He wrote:

> Sometimes you were publicly exposed to insult and persecution; at other times you stood side by side with those who were so treated. You sympathized with those in prison and joyfully accepted the confiscation of your property, because you knew that you yourselves had better and lasting possessions. So do not throw away your confidence; it will be richly rewarded. You need to persevere so that when you have done the will of God, you will receive what he has promised. For in just a very little while, "He who is coming will come and will not delay. But my righteous one will live by faith." (Hebrews 10:33–38)

There's really only one place to go with the big questions—
to the big God who holds in his hands all of eternity. Go ahead, ask
him whatever questions you have. He can handle it.
*Read Habakkuk's gritty conversation with God in the book of Habakkuk.*

# A Royal Prophet

*Zephaniah Doesn't Let His Pedigree Stop Him from
Prophesying Against Judah*

YOUNG MEN related to royalty have a higher expectation of playing
cricket or polo than of prophesying. But Zephaniah didn't fit the
usual expectations of those related to royalty.

Zephaniah could trace his roots back to Hezekiah—the king of
Judah generations previously. The current king, Josiah, was a distant
relative of Zephaniah.

Judah had fallen to the Assyrians, but Josiah's father, Amon,
paid off the Assyrians to keep them from attacking Judah. While
Judah was not physically invaded by Assyrian troops, they were cul-
turally invaded due to the influence of Assyrian politics, fashion,
and religion. Sadly, the complacent people of Judah were unaware
of how bad things were in their hearts.

The Assyrian payoff that King Amon arranged wasn't such a
good deal after all, especially since it angered God. How many
times had God said not to have other gods before him? Yet the Isra-

elites allowed the Assyrian priests into their land—the land that God gave them—and worshipped their gods (mainly Baal and Asherah).

While Josiah tried to make reforms by cleansing the temple in Jerusalem and removing from Judah articles dedicated to the worship of Baal (see 2 Kings 23), evidently the corruption in the land was deeply rooted. So God chose Zephaniah to tell the people of Judah that judgment day was near. Because of their idol worship, people and animals would be destroyed. Not only that, God promised, "On that day I will punish national leaders and sons of the king, along with all who follow foreign customs" (Zephaniah 1:8 CEV).

But this destruction was not exclusive to Israel. Other nations—Assyria, Cush, Moab, and Ammon—would face the fire of God's wrath. Ouch!

Would Zephaniah's relationship to King Josiah (King Amon's son) hurt or help his reputation as God's mouthpiece? Would Zephaniah embarrass the royal family—his family—in order to be obedient to God?

To speak God's message might have seemed treasonous from a human standpoint. But Zephaniah's allegiance was to a higher authority than King Josiah—he answered to the King of the universe. So, Zephaniah spoke as God commanded.

But the message was not all bad. After the time of judgment, there would be a time of rejoicing once the people repented. The King of kings decreed it, and his loyal subject—Zephaniah—spread the word.

*To get the full impact of this prophet's fiery words, read Zephaniah 1–3.*

# If You Build It,
# He Will Come

*God Promises to Show Up if the People Rebuild the Temple*

Priorities—life is full of them. And sometimes the wrong priorities are chosen over the right ones.

Around 586 B.C., the armies of Babylon destroyed the temple in Jerusalem and hauled off most of the Israelites in Judah as their captives. But thousands of exiles were allowed to return to Jerusalem many years later, and they were given permission to rebuild the temple—God's dwelling place and the symbol of his presence. But the people were so happy to be back home that they got a little sidetracked. They decided to get their own houses in order first instead of working on God's house.

After watching them busily consumed by their DIY projects, the Lord decided to send a message through the prophet Haggai: "Is it a time for you yourselves to live in your paneled houses, while this house lies in ruins?" (Haggai 1:4 HCSB).

The people of Judah's problem was confused priorities. Because rebuilding the temple was a low priority for them, they were not blessed with fruitful crops and herds, and they faced drought and dissatisfaction.

Haggai's message did not fall on deaf ears. Like Ray Kinsella (Kevin Costner's character) in the classic *Field of Dreams*, Zerubbabel, the governor of Judah, was stirred to action by the promise "If you build it, he will come." God would be with his people once again.

Zerubbabel gathered a dream team of people committed to the task of building a new temple. One of the team members was Joshua (Jeshua in Ezra 3), a high priest. They came up with a plan and executed it. (To find out how they did, see "Extreme Makeover: Interior Edition," page 95.)

God moved Haggai to speak to the people once again, reminding them of the temple in its former glory. The sad ruins seemed a mockery of a place where the glory of God once rested. But God proposed a temple that someday would have an even greater glory. This temple would not be a building but a person—the Messiah. This Messiah would come through the family line of Zerubbabel.

Rebuilding the temple might have seemed like a field of dreams. How could the returning exiles hope to rebuild what their enemies had destroyed so thoroughly? So God had a final word of encouragement for them: "From this day on I will bless you" (Haggai 2:19 NIV). And although they wouldn't see it in their lifetime, one day God would dwell once again within the temple—the temple of the human body—through the Holy Spirit.

*To find out more about Zerubbabel and his dream team of workers, read Haggai 1–2. See also Ezra 2–3.*

# The King Comes

*Zechariah Prophesies About the Coming Messiah*

SOMETIMES PEOPLE just need a good strong dose of hope. Zechariah the prophet understood this.

To get the full picture of what Zechariah's message of hope meant, here's a long history lesson made short. The Hebrew people who lived in the northern kingdom of Israel had been taken into captivity by the Assyrians. The Assyrians were overthrown by the Babylonians. The Babylonians conquered the southern kingdom of Judah and took the Hebrew people there into captivity. The Babylonians were overthrown by the Medes and Persians. Cyrus, a king of the Medo-Persian empire, allowed the Hebrews in captivity to return to their homeland if they chose to do so.

The books of Ezra and Nehemiah describe the groups of people who took the trek back to their battered homeland. The temple needed to be rebuilt, along with the city wall. The task was daunting. Three men served as prophets during this period—Haggai, Zechariah, and Malachi—and their books appear at the end of the Old Testament. These men ministered to the small but brave remnant of Hebrews who began to rebuild their nation one brick at a time. Zechariah encouraged the people to finish the difficult task of rebuilding the temple—their place of worship, the place where God dwelled among them. Through a series of God-given visions, Zechariah gave the people hope.

One particular vision must have really revved up the people with excitement. The very bricks they were cutting and placing into this new temple would one day be seen by the promised Messiah himself. The city would indeed be rebuilt and would flourish, God promised, and one day, the Messiah would enter its gates. "Rejoice greatly, O daughter of Zion! Shout aloud, O daughter of Jerusalem! Behold, your king is coming to you; righteous and having salvation is he, humble and mounted on a donkey, on a colt, the foal of a donkey" (Zechariah 9:9 ESV).

Fast-forward to five hundred years later. As the Messiah himself prepared to enter the city of Jerusalem, he told his disciples to procure a donkey, thus fulfilling the ancient prophet's words. (See Matthew 21:1–5.)

Zechariah saw more in his oracle—probably more than he could begin to understand. He spoke of how the inhabitants of Jerusalem would "look on me, on him whom they have pierced, they shall mourn for him, as one mourns for an only child, and weep bitterly over him, as one weeps over a firstborn" (Zechariah 12:10). This prophecy was later fulfilled when Jesus hung on the cross: "One of the soldiers pierced his side with a spear, and at once there came out blood and water. . . . For these things took place that the Scripture might be fulfilled: 'Not one of his bones will be broken.' And again another Scripture says, 'They will look on him whom they have pierced'" (John 19:34, 36–37).

And beyond that, Zechariah saw a day when all people will worship the King of kings, a day of joy and gladness.

This prophet brought hope to people who desperately needed it. Readers today look back upon the fulfillment of his words and can also take hope in the prophecies yet to come true.

*To read more about Zechariah's hopeful words about the Messiah, see Zechariah 9.*

# Don't Hold Back

*Malachi Warns the People of Israel to Stop Robbing God*

ACCORDING TO the *American Heritage College Dictionary*, the word *wholehearted* means "marked by unconditional commitment, unstinting devotion, or unreserved enthusiasm." In other words, a wholehearted person holds nothing back, but instead gives his or her all.

This was not a description of the people of Israel in the prophet Malachi's day. In fact, God had another descriptive word: *robbers*. Malachi, the last of the Old Testament prophets, had to call it as God saw it. He began with a brief review of the life and times of Israel.

Israel had a long history of falling away from and returning to the Lord. Fickleness led to a long period of exile, which began when the Babylonians conquered Jerusalem. Decades later, many of the exiles gained permission from Artaxerxes, the king of Persia, to return with leaders like Ezra and Nehemiah and rebuild the walls of Jerusalem, as well as a new temple. Life was on an upswing.

Or was it? The people were discouraged. Where was God? Why had he not returned to fill the temple with his glory as prophets like Haggai had promised? (See "If You Build It, He Will Come," page 165.) When would they ever see the prosperity and redemption that Isaiah prophesied? (See Isaiah 60–66.)

God knew about their grumbling and their feelings of being robbed. But he turned the tables on them. He hadn't rob them—they had robbed him! One aspect of their lack of heart was the way they withheld their tithes and offerings. God wanted his people to wholeheartedly worship him again. Malachi urged the people to stop keeping everything they earned for themselves. The tithes were to be an offering to God, part of which by law the priests and Levites used to support themselves and their families. Because people weren't tithing, the priests had to find other ways to support themselves; thus they weren't fulfilling their priestly duties.

The prophet reminded them that everything they had came from God. What right did they have to keep it all for themselves and not give back 10 percent—all that God required? So, through Malachi, God challenged his people, "Bring the whole tithe into the storehouse, that there may be food in my house. Test me in this . . . and see if I will not throw open the floodgates of heaven and pour out so much blessing that you will not have room enough for it" (Malachi 3:10 NIV).

If the people were obedient, God promised they would have a new name: no longer robbers, but "blessed" (3:12).

*To read about how some of the Israelites robbed God, read Malachi 3.*

# Lunching on Locusts

*John the Baptist Is an Unusual Prophet for an Unusual Time*

Factoids: John the Baptist
- *Domicile:* Judea
- *Date:* Early first century A.D.

- *Occupation:* Prophet
- *Family Ties:* Father, Zechariah; mother, Elizabeth; relative (perhaps cousin), Jesus
- *Mentioned in the Bible:* John's story is told in all four Gospels and in many places throughout the New Testament (see, for example, Acts 1:5, 22; 10:37; 11:16; 13:24–25; 18:25; 19:3–4). His coming was predicted in Isaiah 40:3 and Malachi 4:5.

IN OUR CULTURE, dressing for success involves wearing a fashionable suit or a power tie. But in John the Baptist's day, dressing for success involved a bit more "dressing down"—rough clothes of camel's hair and a leather belt. While that outfit of choice might seem odd, consider the fact that Jesus once said of John, "Truly, I say to you, among those born of women there has arisen no one greater than John the Baptist" (Matthew 11:11 ESV).

Quite a testimony for an unusual and unshakable man.

John was unusual from day one. He had an unusual birth announcement—one delivered by an angel to his disbelieving father, Zechariah. He took the unusual Nazirite vow—a vow that involved no haircutting and the avoidance of fermented drinks. He moved into an unusual neighborhood—the desert. But he also was a man who was "great before the Lord" (Luke 1:15). In other words, he was effective in what God called him to do. His job? To prophesy about the long-awaited coming Messiah, the one who would come in John's lifetime.

John was the "Elijah" promised by the prophet Malachi, whose arrival would bring the hearts of the people back to God (Malachi 4:5). It's fitting that John dressed like the ancient prophet Elijah, who lived nearly nine hundred years earlier. (See 2 Kings 1:8.) He chose to live in the desert, away from distractions, where he could focus on God's instructions. Living the life of a hermit, he ate what God provided in nature. The snack of choice was locusts, with a little touch of honey.

John had a different lifestyle than the religious leaders of his time. He wanted no part of the luxurious houses, flowing robes, and rich foods that reflected the power of their positions as Pharisees and Sadducees. But he earned their ire when he criticized their hypocrisy. (See Matthew 3:7–12.)

John the Baptist's unconventional appearance captured the interest of the people. And once he had their undivided attention, he shared the message from God that carried far more impact than the physical appearance of the messenger. He baptized everyone who repented of their sins and turned to God. He even had the privilege of baptizing the very Messiah he preached about.

Although he was the first genuine prophet of God since Malachi (more than four hundred years earlier), he was humble. Listen to this self-description: "After me will come one more powerful than I, the thongs of whose sandals I am not worthy to stoop down and untie. I baptize you with water, but he will baptize you with the Holy Spirit" (Mark 1:7–8 NIV).

John's whole purpose in life was to bring others to Jesus. He was "a voice of one calling in the desert" (1:3), pointing the way to new life. Not bad for someone who wore camel's hair and ate locusts.

*For more about John the Baptist's eccentric look and powerful message, read Matthew 3; Mark 1:1–11; Luke 3; and John 1.*

PART FIVE

# Freaks and Greeks

# King-Sized King

*A Fat King Is Tricked by a Left-Handed Judge*

Factoids: Ehud
- *Domicile:* Canaan
- *Date:* Sometime between 1380 B.C. and 1050 B.C.
- *Occupation:* Messenger, judge
- *Family Ties:* Father, Gera the Benjamite
- *Mentioned in the Bible:* Judges 3:12–30

THIS STORY BEGINS with an unfortunate recurring theme: "Once again, the Israelites did evil in the sight of the LORD" (Judges 3:12 NIV). So the Lord sent judgment. After forty years of relative peace, Eglon, the king of Moab, decided to increase his territory and power. His armies attacked Israel and, because of their wickedness, Israel was defeated. Not only did they lose the battle, they became subject to Eglon for the next eighteen years.

Enter our hero, Ehud. He was from the tribe of Benjamin and was God's chosen deliverer. When he was sent to King Eglon, he had a little plan up his sleeve . . . or on his right thigh, to be exact.

What may seem strange to some is that the Bible actually mentions the fact that Ehud was a southpaw, a "left-handed man" (3:15). It also mentions that King Eglon "was a very fat man" (3:17). What could possibly be so important about one man's being left-handed and another's being obese that historians included it in the biblical record?

First of all, King Eglon didn't gain his weight feasting on the harvest from his own personal farm. Rather, as was custom of the time, he gorged himself on the tributes brought by those who were subject to him. A conquering king would exact the first fruits—the best produce and flocks—from those whom he ruled. This accomplished two objectives: it kept the king and his army well fed, and it weakened those who might rebel against him. After all, if they had only enough food for subsistence, they would never have the energy to fight back. For Eglon, this system worked well for eighteen years.

Second, thanks to his uniqueness, Ehud was able to end Eglon's reign. Being left-handed in Ehud's day was considered a handicap. When he was sent with the tribute (the first fruits) to Eglon, he was probably searched for a hidden weapon. If he had been right-handed, a sword would be strapped to his left side. No one would think to check his right side for a hidden sword. Thus he was able to sneak the deadly item past the guards when he went in to speak to Eglon alone.

Ehud was used by God to free the people of Israel from an oppressive, greedy king. By saying, "I have a secret message for you, O king" (3:19), Ehud was able to secure a private meeting with Eglon. When they were alone, Ehud gave his "pointed" message to the king, who found himself on the receiving end of Ehud's double-edged sword. Ehud then escaped by calmly strolling out and locking the door.

The assassination and subsequent escape could not have happened without the hand of God, the real king-sized King of the universe. When Ehud later led his people into battle against the Moabites, the Israelites defeated their enemies. They were back on top—until the next crisis.

*To read about this "lefty," go to Judges 3:12–30.*

# A Strong
# Man's Weakness

*Samson's Strength Becomes His Achilles' Heel*

Factoids: Samson
- *Domicile:* Zorah, Timnah, Ashkelon, Gaza, Valley of Sorek
- *Date:* Around 1075 to 1055 B.C.
- *Occupation:* Judge of Israel
- *Family Ties:* Father, Manoah
- *Mentioned in the Bible:* Judges 13–16; Hebrews 11:32

REMEMBER ACHILLES? He was a hero in Greek mythology who fought in the Trojan War. Achilles was invincible in battle except for one little tiny spot, way down near his foot. His heel was the only vulnerable part of his body, and of course, that was the very spot that his enemies exploited to kill him. Well, Samson was a hero in ancient Hebrew history, who learned too late that he had an Achilles' heel.

Samson was set apart by God at birth. His mother had been unable to conceive for many years. One day an angel appeared to her and told her she would have a son who would be a Nazirite, which meant taking a vow that included no wine and no haircutting. Samson would be one of a long line of handpicked deliverers known as judges who fought against Israel's enemies. Like Achilles, he would be tested in battle. But he would have strength to match that of another fabled Greek hero, Hercules.

Sadly, Samson was not strong in his convictions. Sure, he could tear apart a lion with his bare hands, but he always picked women who were wrong for him, and he attempted to play mind games with the Philistines—the enemies of Israel and the people he was charged to defeat.

Having selected a Philistine wife, against his parents' wishes, Samson decided to make sport of his wife's townspeople with a riddle related to the lion he killed. If they could guess the riddle, he would give them thirty new outfits, including thirty items made of linen—undoubtedly a wardrobe to die for. If they couldn't guess it, they would have to give the items to Samson.

When they couldn't guess the riddle, the Philistines threatened to kill Samson's wife and her family. Obviously there were some sore losers in town. The woman begged Samson to tell her the riddle, which she then explained to her people. Samson lost his temper and killed thirty Philistines to gain their clothing in payment. He also gave away his wife. Samson's experience with his Philistine wife foreshadowed a relationship that would lead to his doom—his relationship with Delilah.

The Philistine leaders approached Delilah with an offer she couldn't refuse: find out what made Samson strong. A handsome reward would be hers. Delilah agreed.

So much for standing by your man.

When Samson finally gave away his secret, Delilah called in a man to give Samson his first and only haircut. When Samson woke up, he didn't realize that the spirit of the Lord had departed. He was quickly taken into captivity by the Philistines. They decided to make an example of him by depriving him of his eyesight and forcing him to grind grain in the prison.

But God had mercy on his wayward deliverer. One of the most promising verses in this sad account is 16:22: "Before long, his hair began to grow back."

Obviously firm believers in the "kick a man when he's down" school of thought, the Philistines decided to have a laugh at Samson's expense. Samson was taken to the temple where all could see and mock the fallen hero.

But God had the last laugh. After Samson requested that he be placed by the pillars of the temple, God brought the house down with a display of strength—the final act of Samson's life.

This hero was no longer a zero.

*To learn more about Samson's loves and locks, read Judges 13–16.*

# A Giant Problem

*Goliath the Giant Is Cut Down to Size by Pint-Sized David*

Factoids: Goliath
- *Domicile:* Gath, a city in Philistia
- *Date:* Around 1025 B.C.
- *Occupation:* Mercenary, soldier
- *Family Ties:* Brother, Lahmi
- *Mentioned in the Bible:* 1 Samuel 17; 21:9; 22:10; 2 Samuel 21:19; 1 Chronicles 20:5

Factoids: David
- *Domicile:* Bethlehem, Jerusalem
- *Date:* Around 1025 B.C.

- *Occupation:* Shepherd, musician, poet, soldier, king
- *Family Ties:* Father, Jesse; seven brothers, including Eliab, Abinadab, and Shammah; many wives, including Michal, Ahinoam, Bathsheba, and Abigail; many sons, including Absalom, Amnon, Solomon, and Adonijah; many daughters, including Tamar
- *Mentioned in the Bible:* 1 Samuel 16–1 Kings 2; 1 Chronicles 10–29; Amos 6:5; Matthew 1:1, 6; 22:43–45; Luke 1:32; 2:4; Acts 13:22; Romans 1:3; Hebrews 11:32

S TORIES OF GIANTS are usually confined to fairy tales compiled by the Brothers Grimm or Andrew Lang. We don't expect them to crop up in the Bible. But they do.

Goliath was a giant, but not a friendly one like the Jolly Green Giant or the eponymous Big Friendly Giant of Roald Dahl's classic book *The BFG.*

During this time in Israel's history, relations with the Philistines were often hostile. When Saul's army first saw the Philistine champion Goliath, they must have been shaking in their armor. The sight of a man more than 9 feet tall whose chain mail alone weighed about 125 pounds would inspire fear in any person. Obviously, he was a force to be reckoned with!

As was the custom of the day, in order to avoid the high cost of battle (in lost lives and damaged weapons), each side would send out their strongest fighting man. The winner of this two-man contest would be considered the winner of the battle. Knowing this, the Philistines made a brilliant military move by sending out a man who could defeat most men. But they weren't counting on God's joining the battle. God had a champion as well, albeit an unlikely one.

David was the youngest of eight sons of Jesse, the oldest of which were soldiers in Saul's army. He was usually to be found in the fields watching the family's sheep. But on this day Jesse sent David to the encampment with food for his brothers and their superiors.

At the camp David couldn't miss Goliath, especially after hearing his taunts. Goliath dared to trash-talk the God of Israel and no one but David seemed to take offense. None of the soldiers was willing to challenge Goliath, and Saul certainly wasn't stepping up to the plate.

David's solution: *he* would fight Goliath.

What a difference a little perspective can make.

While the Israelite soldiers saw an unconquerable foe, David saw a human being in direct defiance of God Almighty.

While David's oldest brother, Eliab, put David down for what he assumed was empty boasting, King Saul was flabbergasted at the thought of the young shepherd fighting (and most likely losing to) a seasoned warrior. But he had no other options.

It took young David to remind Saul where real strength came from: "The LORD who delivered me from the paw of the lion and the paw of the bear will deliver me from the hand of this Philistine" (1 Samuel 17:37 NIV).

At this, Saul gave David his blessing and his armor. But David chose to go to battle unarmored and with just a slingshot and some stones.

What a sight small David must have seemed to huge Goliath. A mere youth against a mighty man of battle! But this mere youth picked up a stone and began his slingshot windup, uttering the chilling statement, "I come against you in the name of the LORD Almighty" (17:45). Goliath soon learned that big defeats can come in small packages.

This story ended with a stone launched from the sling of David into the forehead of Goliath. Soon Goliath was dead.

Unfortunately, defeating Goliath eventually caused giant problems for David, and placed him squarely on Saul's most wanted list. But the God who could solve all giant problems was with him.

*To read about the confrontation between David and Goliath, read 1 Samuel 17.*

# Animal Attraction

*Nebuchadnezzar Goes Mad and Becomes like an Animal*

Factoids: Nebuchadnezzar
- *Domicile:* Babylon
- *Date:* Around 550 B.C.
- *Occupation:* King of Babylon
- *Family Ties:* Father, Nabopolasser; son, Evil-Merodach; grandson, Belshazzar
- *Mentioned in the Bible:* 2 Kings 24–25; 2 Chronicles 36; Jeremiah 21–52; Daniel 1–4

THE BIGGER THEY ARE, the harder they fall.

Nebuchadnezzar was the king of Babylon and the commander of a force that conquered nations. He lived in a beautiful palace and thought of himself as king of the world.

But Nebuchadnezzar had a strange dream that troubled him. In the dream was a magnificent tree brimming with fruit that animals and birds feasted upon. But suddenly a voice called for the tree to be cut down, leaving only a stump.

The voice continued to describe what was in store for the stump. It would be bound in chains. But soon the voice seemed to talk about a person, rather than just a tree stump. This person's mind would become like that of an animal until an allotted time passed. He would live outside just as the animals lived.

None of the king's advisers could interpret this dream, until Daniel (or Belteshazzar, as he was known in Babylon) showed up.

Daniel had successfully interpreted a previous dream of Nebuchadnezzar (see Daniel 2). Could he do so again?

Reluctantly, Daniel provided the interpretation he received from God. The tree was Nebuchadnezzar and he was about to be cut down. But his kingdom would remain until Nebuchadnezzar learned his lesson.

Daniel's prophetic words soon came to pass. One afternoon, Nebuchadnezzar went for a stroll on the palace roof. Impressed by all he surveyed, he declared, "Is not this great Babylon, which I have built by my mighty power as a royal residence and for the glory of my majesty?" (Daniel 4:30 NIV).

Having just patted himself on the back, he suddenly heard a voice from heaven: "You will be driven away from people and will live with the wild animals" (4:32).

And immediately it came to pass. The once proud king of the world completely lost his mind. He chomped grass and crawled about as if he were an animal.

But, as per the dream, Nebuchadnezzar's mind and kingdom were restored to him after the time God allotted passed. Rather than being angry at God because of the bout of insanity, Nebuchadnezzar praised him. Deeply humbled, he resumed his reign.

Indeed "pride comes before destruction, a haughty spirit before a fall" (Proverbs 16:18).

*To read about Nebuchadnezzar's four-footed, grass-eating experience, see Daniel 4.*

## Non-Jews Who Believed in God

| Person | Who He/She Was | Reference |
| --- | --- | --- |
| Melchizedek | King of Salem (Jerusalem) and priest of God Most High; met and blessed Abraham | Genesis 14:17–20 |
| Jethro | Moses's father-in-law and priest of Midian; helped Moses learn to delegate his responsibilities as judge of the people | Exodus 2:15–3:1, 4:18; 18:1–27 |
| Naaman | Commander of the army of the king of Aram (Syria); healed of leprosy when the prophet Elisha told him to wash himself seven times in the Jordan River | 2 Kings 5:1–19 |
| Cyrus | King of Persia; allowed the Jews who had been taken into captivity by the Babylonians to return to their homeland and rebuild | 2 Chronicles 36:22–23; Ezra 1:1–4 |
| Nebuchadnezzar | King of Babylon; after some time spent in insanity, decided that Daniel's God alone was the one true God; unknown if Nebuchadnezzar remained a believer | Daniel 4:34–37 |
| King and people of Nineveh | Turned to God at the words of Jonah the prophet | Jonah 3:5–9 |
| Roman centurion | Career military officer commanding more than one hundred men; believed that Jesus could heal his servant even at a distance; his faith amazed and pleased Jesus | Matthew 8:5–13; Luke 7:1–10 |
| Luke | Gentile physician; author of the Gospel of Luke and the book of Acts; traveled with Paul | Acts 1:1–4; 16–28; Colossians 4:14 |
| Ethiopian eunuch | Treasurer of Candace, queen of the Ethiopians; traveled to Jerusalem to worship, was met by Philip, and became a believer in Christ | Acts 8:26–39 |

| Person | Who He/She Was | Reference |
|--------|----------------|-----------|
| Cornelius | Roman centurion; God sent Peter to bring the gospel message to him—a new concept to Peter, who didn't understand that Gentiles, too, could become Christians. Cornelius and his family believed and the Holy Spirit came upon them | Acts 10:1–11:18 |

# Waiting on Widows

*The Greek Widows in the Early Church Gain Assistance*

WHEN WE THINK of the apostles—those stalwart disciples of Jesus—the word *waiter* usually does not immediately come to mind. But it figures prominently in the story of the Greek widows.

After Pentecost, when the Holy Spirit arrived to stay, many people became believers. They were witnesses to miracles and generously shared their belongings with those in need.

With such a spiritual high, a spiritual low was inevitable. Persecution became the main order of the day as the Jewish council tried to force believers to stop preaching in the name of Jesus. But the believers continued to band together.

The early church had its share of internal issues. In the early Jerusalem church, issues were arising as a result of the language barrier. The church was made up of Hebraic Christian Jews who spoke

Aramaic, and Grecian Christian Jews who spoke Greek. The Greek Christians complained to the apostles about their widows—they weren't given food like the others. This was probably not an intentional slight but rather a communication breakdown.

Keeping their priorities straight, the apostles recognized that their primary job in the early church was to preach the word. They observed, "It would not be right for us to neglect the ministry of the word of God in order to wait on tables" (Acts 6:2 NIV). Yet this administrative job was not taken lightly. There needed to be people put in charge of this vital ministry to the widows. So how did they go about finding the right men?

Notice the prerequisites for administrating the food program. They had to choose seven men who were full of the Holy Spirit and wise. These men would carry the responsibility of assisting many widows on a daily basis and would have to work with people closely as they broke through the language and cultural barriers.

Seven respected men who met the requirements were chosen for the job. Stephen, Philip, Procorus, Nicanor, Timon, Parmenas, and Nicolas were presented to the apostles, who prayed for them and laid hands on them. Laying hands on someone was an ancient Jewish practice that signified the setting apart of someone for special service to God. (See Numbers 27:23 and Deuteronomy 34:9.) These men were commissioned to run this vital program of the church.

Just because these seven men weren't preachers didn't make their job less important. They were Spirit-filled and wise and took on the responsibility for an area that needed good administration. They served the church well.

*The story of the hungry widows and the servant-deacons is found in Acts 6:1–6.*

# Timothy Takes a Trip

*Timothy Leaves All to Follow Paul*

Factoids: Timothy
- *Domicile:* Lystra
- *Date:* Sometime after A.D. 63
- *Occupation:* Missionary; pastor
- *Family Ties:* Greek father (unnamed); mother, Eunice; grandmother, Lois
- *Mentioned in the Bible:* Acts 16:1–3; Romans 16:21; 1 Corinthians 4:17; 16:10–11; 2 Corinthians 1:1, 19; Philippians 1:1, 2:19–23; Colossians 1:1; 1 Thessalonians 1:1; 3:2–6; 2 Thessalonians 1:1; 1 and 2 Timothy; Philemon 1; Hebrews 13:23

L IFE CAN CHANGE unexpectedly at the drop of a hat. Sometimes it just takes a visit from a compelling person to cause one to long for a change. Paul was that compelling person in Timothy's life.

A missionary to the Gentiles, Paul often traveled with an entourage. Barnabas, one of the first Christians to encourage him in the faith (after Ananias—see Acts 9), traveled with him to such locales as Cyprus, Perga, Pisidian Antioch, Iconium, Lystra, and Derbe. But as is the case with many human pairings, even Christian ones, problems arose. A disagreement over John Mark (the writer of the Gospel of Mark) caused Paul and Barnabas to go their separate ways.

But the work of the gospel continued. As Paul traveled to the cities he previously visited, he returned to Lystra. There he met Timothy, a half-Greek believer, who was probably a teenager at this point. Timothy was Greek on his father's side. His mother, Eunice, was Jewish.

Evidently, there was something about Timothy that impressed Paul. For one thing, the other believers had good things to say about him. Paul provided a second clue in his letter to Timothy: "Remembering your tears, I long to see you so that I may be filled with joy, clearly recalling your sincere faith that first lived in your grandmother Lois, then in your mother Eunice, and that I am convinced is in you also" (2 Timothy 1:4–5 HCSB).

Timothy's mother and grandmother had an impact on Timothy's spiritual life, one that led Paul to make Timothy part of the missionary team. But Timothy had not been circumcised. This was the issue Peter once discussed with the Jewish council in Jerusalem (see Acts 11:1–3), and which sparked a later debate within the same group (see Acts 15:1–35). Although circumcision was not necessary to prove one's faith, Paul knew that the Jews in the area to which they would be traveling would be offended if Timothy avoided this rite. So Paul took care of the circumcision.

Just as Jesus' disciples left everything behind to follow him, so Timothy left all to follow Paul on a missionary adventure that had many ups and downs, thanks to Paul's tendency to find trouble wherever he went. Later, when Timothy became the overseer of the church at Ephesus, Paul wrote two letters to encourage the young leader, whom he called "my true child in the faith" (1 Timothy 1:2). Not a bad recommendation for a sincere young man.

*To read more about Timothy's journeys with Paul, go to Acts 16:1–3. See also 1 and 2 Timothy.*

# My Big Fat
# Greek Adventure

*Paul Makes His Way Through Macedonia*

Factoids: Paul
- *Domicile:* Born in Tarsus, but had no known residence after becoming a missionary
- *Date:* Sometime between A.D. 49–52
- *Occupation:* Missionary; tentmaker; former member of the Jewish council (Sanhedrin)
- *Family Ties:* Unknown
- *Mentioned in the Bible:* Acts 7:58–28:31, and throughout his New Testament letters

THE LIFE OF THE APOSTLE PAUL would make a great series of action movies. Driving out demons, raising the dead, running from the authorities, singing in jail, dealing with death threats—life doesn't get more exciting!

Many great hero stories begin with a call to action. Paul's call came through a vision he had one night of a man who told him, "Come over to Macedonia and help us" (Acts 16:9 ESV). Since this vision came after Paul and his traveling companions were prevented by the Holy Spirit from going to another location, Paul knew that God was leading him to Macedonia. Oopa!

Back in the day, Macedonia had a reputation for military might, thanks to Philip II and Alexander the Great. As Paul prepared to reach Macedonia for the sake of Christ, the territory was under Roman rule. But Greek was still spoken throughout Macedonia.

The first major stop on the Macedonian tour was Philippi, a city named after Philip II. There, Paul and his companions, who included Silas and Timothy, met Lydia, a businesswoman from Thyatira. She had the distinction of being the first Macedonian converted to Christianity.

After the triumph of bringing Lydia into the kingdom of God and being invited to share her hospitality, trouble was sure to follow. It came in the form of a demon-possessed slave girl who acted as the unofficial public relations person for Paul and Silas with her continual announcements that Paul and Silas were men of God.

The girl's words were hardly flattering and were in fact problematic. Paul put a stop to the announcements by casting the spirit out of the girl. Since the demon helped the girl tell fortunes, that source of income was now gone. In retaliation, the girl's owners had Paul and Silas arrested, beaten, and thrown into prison. (Read that story in "Not for Profit Prophet," page 192.)

Instead of moping in prison, Paul and Silas praised God! Suddenly, there was an earthquake, which cracked the foundation of the prison.

The frightened jailer feared a prison break and tried to commit suicide. But Paul and Silas assured him that no one had escaped. The grateful jailer then asked the words that many others later asked—"Sirs, what must I do to be saved?" (16:30). The jailer believed in Jesus as per Paul and Silas's advice. His whole family also believed.

When the city officials arrived the next day to release Paul and Silas, Paul explained that, as Roman citizens, Silas and he should not have been beaten without going through trial. They couldn't leave the city fast enough for the officials.

On to Thessalonica—the capital of Macedonia and the center of more trouble for Paul and Silas. After Paul and Silas preached about Jesus, envious Jews instigated a group to start a riot. The presence of Paul and Silas gained their host, Jason, a trip before the city leaders and a stiff fine because of the riot.

On to Berea, where Paul and Silas met a group of believers eager to study the Scriptures. Being with the Bereans was a nice respite, especially when many important Greek citizens joined the family of God. But trouble soon followed when rabblerousers from Thessalonica arrived in Berea. While Silas and Timothy remained in Berea, Paul went on to Athens, where he debated with renowned Greek philosophers in the Areopagus. Later, after traveling in Ephesus, Paul returned to Macedonia, after narrowly escaping a group of Jews who wished to kill him. All in a day's work for Paul!

During a particularly long sermon Paul preached at Troas, a young man named Eutychus grew sleepy and fell out of a window and died. Amazingly, that was not the end for Eutychus. After Paul placed himself on Eutychus, Eutychus came back to life! Needless to say, that made a huge impact on the crowd.

These were just some of triumphs and tragedies of Paul's big fat Greek adventure. Paul, the world's most unwitting action star, went on to face many more perils throughout his missionary adventures.

*To read more about Paul's amazing adventures throughout Macedonia, read Acts 16:6–20:38.*

# Not for Profit Prophet

*Paul Is Arrested for Healing a Demon-Possessed Girl*

DEMONS APPARENTLY can't keep their mouths shut. Throughout Jesus' earthly ministry, when unclean spirits came into his presence, they immediately knew who he really was and would start yelling, "Here he is! This is the Holy One! Look out! He's the one who will cast us into utter darkness forever!" They'd shriek and torment the person they were occupying at the time, throwing him or her around like a rag doll, flinging saliva and curses in every direction until Jesus would firmly and authoritatively silence them. The ominous quiet that would ensue filled everyone with awe and made as much of an impression as the loud noises the demon interlopers had been making seconds before.

The same thing happened at times to the apostles. Filled with the Holy Spirit of God, they would go about their business in far-flung corners of the Roman Empire, often where the gospel had not yet been preached. In such places demonic spirits "ruled" whole swaths of human territory unchallenged. When Spirit-filled men like Paul or Peter appeared, the demons immediately sensed that their own days were numbered. But they could never keep quiet. They had to blab out what they knew. "These men are servants of the Most High God, who are telling you the way to be saved" (Acts 16:17 NIV), cried out one demon who inhabited the body of a little slave girl who followed Paul and Silas around in the streets of the Philippi.

Now, at first glimpse of these stories, we might think, *Hey, it's free publicity. What's the problem? Let the demons talk.* But this was hardly the kind of advertisement they needed. Paul finally became very annoyed by the constant yelling of the demon who possessed the slave girl and through her gave accurate predictions about the future. Such an ability is sought after in the marketplaces of the world, so her owners were turning a tidy profit by the "prophecies" of this diviner-soothsayer slave girl.

Paul, though, got tired of the constant demonic voice, like a carnival huckster, bringing attention to Paul and his companions. Not to mention that it was pretty awful for the poor slave girl who was possessed. So one day Paul whirled around to face the girl who followed them, and he simply said, "Okay, that's it. We're done here. In the name of the Lord Jesus Christ, I command you to come out of her." And indeed, the spirit was gone, instantly.

The spirit in the slave girl had prophesied truly. What Paul and Silas were proclaiming in the homes and streets and prison of Philippi was indeed the way of salvation. Those who believed that message were saved and given a new life.

*To read more about this demon-defeating event, read Acts 16:16–18.*

# Let the Areopagus Games Begin

*Dionysius and Damaris Become Believers*

ATHENS IS CONSIDERED the birthplace of Western civilization and culture. In the first century it was a very advanced city compared to others in the region. One of the main pastimes was discussing the latest ideas (see Acts 17:21). Epicurean and Stoic philosophers thrived there. While Epicureans pursued pleasure, Stoics taught self-control. The conflict between having fun and showing self-restraint was in full swing.

The apostle Paul couldn't help thinking about the vast array of gods worshipped in ancient Greece. While Paul waited for fellow missionaries Silas and Timothy to join him in the city, he was confronted with a plethora of idols. There was even a shrine inscribed "To the Unknown God." Undoubtedly, the people of Athens wanted to cover all the bases.

The large number of idols and shrines in Athens really bothered Paul, so he decided to do something about it. He began debating with the Jews and Gentiles in the synagogue. He also had interesting discussions with the Epicurean and Stoic philosophers, who didn't know what to make of Paul. Was he crazy? Did he want to start a new religion? The forum for their discussions was the Areopagus—a place named after Ares, the Greek god of war and thunder. Here, some of the greatest philosophers of the day waited to hear what this Jewish preacher had to say.

The forum didn't intimidate a well-educated master of apologetics like Paul. As usual, he made a good case for the gospel of Jesus Christ, explaining the value of worshipping a God who could be known. This God was the Father of all who believed in the Son—Jesus.

Paul's message received mixed reviews. While some mocked him, others wanted to hear more. There is a vast difference between hearing a message and believing it. Many of the erudite philosophers listened politely to his arguments but couldn't be bothered with silly things such as someone being raised from the dead.

We know that at least a few Athenians accepted the message of Jesus that Paul taught. Two of them were Dionysius and Damaris. Dionysius was a member of the council of philosophers who met at the Areopagus. Pretty amazing that a council member believed! No other facts are mentioned about Damaris other than that she was a woman. Was she a well-known person in Athens? A woman of means? Did she become a comissionary or church leader later?

Regardless of what these two Greek believers did for the church, the fact remains that they both not only heard the message but also believed it. And that made a world of difference.

*To learn more about Paul's adventures in the Areopagus, read Acts 17:15–34.*

# A Gentile
# in the Synagogue

*Titius Justus, a Gentile, Adds to the Diversity of the Church*

When life hands you lemons, make lemonade." The apostle Paul lived many centuries before this modern idiom came into play. But he certainly lived out that advice.

Being a missionary was Paul's first job, but his day job was making tents—a skill he put to use to support himself. While in Corinth, he met some fellow tentmakers—Priscilla and her husband, Aquila—who were believers as well. They became coworkers in every sense of the word.

Every Sabbath, Paul preached in the synagogue, trying to convince both Jews and Greeks (Gentiles) that Jesus was the long-awaited Messiah. The Jews, however, refused to listen and even fought against Paul. After shaking his robe at them—an action akin to shaking the dust off one's feet, Paul told them, "Your blood be on your own heads! I am clear of my responsibility. From now on I will go to the Gentiles" (Acts 18:6 NIV). In other words, you made your bed of unbelief—now lie in it. Paul was ready to move on to the specific call God had given him—preaching to the Gentiles.

When Paul became a believer, God chose him "to carry [his] name before the Gentiles and their kings and before the people of Israel" (Acts 9:15). Paul was about to take the lemons of the rejection of his people and make lemonade by focusing on the Gentiles.

Because Paul spent so much time at the synagogue, he met many of the residents of the area. One of them was Titius Justus, a Gentile who lived next door to the synagogue and worshipped God. Another was Crispus, the synagogue ruler, who became a believer. Like Titius, Crispus was a Gentile.

Because hospitality was customary, Titius invited Paul to stay in his home. But the apostle Peter had fallen into trouble with Jewish believers just for visiting a Gentile believer named Cornelius (see Acts 11:1–2, and "A Voice to the Gentiles" on page 110). After all, for many years the Jews did not believe associating with Gentiles was permissible by law. Now Paul was about to go one step further than Peter had by living in the home of a Gentile!

It is believed that Titius is probably the "Gaius Paul" mentioned in Paul's letter to the Romans: "Gaius, whose hospitality I and the whole church here enjoy" (Romans 16:23). By offering hospitality to Paul and other missionaries, Titius shared in the privilege of spreading the gospel.

Being rejected by his own people was difficult for Paul. But the positive response of Gentiles like Titius and Crispus undoubtedly encouraged Paul and helped change the face of the church.

*To read more about Paul's new friends in Corinth, see Acts 18:1–17.*

## THE PEOPLE PAUL ENCOUNTERED

Paul met many, many people during his missionary journeys. Some encounters were better than others.

| PERSON | REFERENCE | PLACE/EVENT |
|---|---|---|
| Bar-Jesus, a false prophet and sorcerer also known as Elymas | Acts 13:6–12 | While traveling through Paphos in Cyprus, Paul and Barnabas tangled with Elymas, who tried to undermine their witness before a proconsul—Sergius Paulus. |

| PERSON | REFERENCE | PLACE/EVENT |
|---|---|---|
| Lydia, a businesswoman ("seller of purple goods"—Acts 16:14 ESV) | Acts 16:13–15 | Paul and Silas met Lydia in Philippi, where Lydia became the first Macedonian convert. |
| Demon-possessed slave girl | Acts 16:16–40 | Casting a demon out of a fortune-telling slave girl led to imprisonment for Paul and Silas. |
| Philippian jailer | Acts 16:25–35 | The jailer became a believer after Paul and Silas refused to escape after an earthquake rocked the foundation of the prison. |
| Jason | Acts 17:5–9 | Paul stayed in Jason's home in Thessalonica. After a riot caused by the Jews' jealous reaction to Paul's preaching, Jason had to post bond. |
| Epicurean and Stoic philosophers | Acts 17:18–34 | In Athens, Paul debated with famed philosophers over an unknown God and a God who could be known—Jesus. |
| Dionysius and Damaris | Acts 17:32–34 | After debating among Greek philosophers, Paul welcomed these two converts to the family of God. |
| Titius Justus | Acts 18:7–9 | This Gentile who lived next door to the synagogue became a believer when Paul preached there, and welcomed Paul into his home. |
| Crispus | Acts 18:7–9 | This synagogue leader became a believer, along with his household, after meeting Paul in Corinth. |

| PERSON | REFERENCE | PLACE/EVENT |
|---|---|---|
| Seven sons of Sceva | Acts 19:13–16 | Seven sons of a Jewish priest were beaten severely after trying to cast out demons "in the name of Jesus whom Paul preaches" (Acts 19:13 NIV). |
| Eutychus | Acts 20:7–12 | In Troas this young man fell asleep during one of Paul's sermons and fell to his death out of window, but Paul brought him back to life through the power of the Holy Spirit. |
| Antonius Felix, the Roman governor of Judea | Acts 24 | Felix presided over Paul's sedition trial in Caesarea. When Paul did not give him a bribe, Felix left Paul in prison. |
| Festus | Acts 25 | The governor of Judea after Felix agreed to send Paul to Rome after Paul appealed to Caesar. |
| King Agrippa II | Acts 25:13–26:32 | When Paul preached the gospel of before Agrippa during the king's visit to Caesarea, Agrippa pronounced him insane. |
| Publius, chief official on the island of Malta | Acts 28:7–10 | While shipwrecked, Paul enjoyed the hospitality of Publius and healed Publius's father. |
| Philemon and Onesimus | The letter to Philemon | After meeting Paul the runaway slave, Onesimus, became a Christian and was urged to return to his master, Philemon. |

# The Dynamic Duo

*Priscilla and Aquila Join Paul's Missionary Entourage*

Factoids: Priscilla and Aquila
- *Domicile:* Corinth
- *Date:* Around A.D. 49–52
- *Occupation:* Missionaries, tentmakers
- *Family Ties:* They were married to each other
- *Mentioned in the Bible:* Acts 18:1–3 and 18–26; Romans 16:3–5; 1 Corinthians 16:19; 2 Timothy 4:19

WHEN A "DYNAMIC DUO" is mentioned, many think of Batman and Robin. But the Bible has its share of dynamic duos—people whose teamwork aided a noble cause. Priscilla and Aquila are such a duo.

During a time of great persecution, many Christians were forced out of Rome by the emperor, Claudius. Aquila and his wife, Priscilla (also known as Prisca), headed to Corinth, where they made one of the most important friendships of their lives—with the famed apostle Paul.

Aquila and Priscilla had two things in common with Paul: they were believers, and they were tentmakers by trade. Paul stayed and worked with them. Their companionship was undoubtedly comforting while he talked each week with Jews and Greeks in the local synagogue.

Later, Paul sailed with Priscilla and Aquila to Ephesus, where he again took up his habit of preaching in synagogues. But when Paul moved on, Priscilla and Aquila remained in Ephesus.

It's interesting that whenever Priscilla and Aquila are mentioned in the Bible, Priscilla's name comes first—not a common occurrence among husbands and wives. Perhaps Priscilla was better known than her husband for some reason.

When Apollos, a preacher from Alexandria, arrived in Ephesus and began to share his knowledge of God, Priscilla and Aquila realized that Apollos lacked something vital: a fuller knowledge of Jesus. He knew only about what John the Baptist had to say about Jesus, but nothing about the Holy Spirit or the fact that Jesus died and was resurrected. Rather than call him out in public, they invited him home and tactfully taught him about Jesus.

These two were always bringing people home and encouraging them. At some point, Priscilla and Aquila must have returned to Rome. There they opened their home for believers to meet on a regular basis.

In keeping with the dynamic duo job description, Priscilla and Aquila were risk takers and lifesavers. When writing letters to the Christians in and around Rome, Paul had this to say about Priscilla and Aquila: "Give my greetings to Prisca and Aquila, my co-workers in Christ Jesus, who risked their own necks for my life. Not only do I thank them, but so do all the Gentile churches" (Romans 16:3–4 HCSB). Since they had a quieter ministry, they might not have been as flashy and well-known as Paul, but they were just as memorable.

*To read more about this husband-and-wife team, read Acts 18:1–3 and 18–26.*

# All for One
# and One for All

*Paul Urges a Friend to Help Euodia and Syntyche Repair Their Broken Friendship*

TWO BRICKS in a building and an Oreo cookie. What do these two things have in common? They're held together by the stuff between them. In the case of the bricks, you find the mortar that bonds one brick to another. The Oreo cookie has the all-important white filling.

The apostle Paul once asked a friend to be the mortar or filling between two women. Why? Because they just weren't getting along.

Paul's job as an apostle was to "plant" churches. Later, he "watered" them through the spiritual teaching in his letters, which served as Paul's voice when he couldn't visit in person. In fact, he wrote to the church in the Roman colony of Philippi while he was in prison.

In the midst of this letter about joy, Paul sadly had to address the disharmony between two women, Euodia and Syntyche. Fearing that these women would not work out the problem on their own, he enlisted the help of a third party.

Not much is known about this man except that he was a "loyal yokefellow" (Philippians 4:3 NIV). This image brings to mind two beasts of burden linked together under a common yoke. He was someone who worked closely with Paul, and perhaps was a leader in the church in Philippi. This man would now be an important part of this mission to patch up the disagreement.

When tension happens within a church body, everybody is affected. Imagine being the one charged with the task of bringing two angry women face-to-face. With a sticky problem like this, some people might have hesitated to get involved out of fear of being caught in the cross fire. So Paul had to call for a volunteer. This may have been an assignment for which Paul's friend was perfectly suited, or it may have been a dreaded chore. Nevertheless, Paul felt that he was the one who could help these two irate women patch up their differences.

The text never reveals the outcome of the intervention of Paul's yokefellow. But this story illustrates the truth that in the church, like Alexandre Dumas's three musketeers, it's "all for one, and one for all."

*To read about this little spat in the early church, read Philippians 4:2–3.*

# The Twelve Tasks
# of Titus

*Titus Has a Lengthy To-do List as the Leader of the Church in Crete*

Factoids: Titus
- *Domicile:* From somewhere in Greece; went as Paul's emissary to the churches in Corinth and on the island of Crete
- *Date:* Around A.D. 64
- *Occupation:* Missionary
- *Family Ties:* Parents were Gentiles
- *Mentioned in the Bible:* 2 Corinthians 2:13; 7:6–7, 13; 8:6, 16, 23; 12:18; Galatians 2:1–3; 2 Timothy 4:10; Titus 1:4

IN GREEK MYTHOLOGY, the famed hero Hercules had twelve great tasks, known as "the labors of Hercules." These tasks were ones that no ordinary man could perform. But even ordinary men are sometimes called to perform heroic feats. Take, for example, the to-do list Paul assigned to Titus. With about a dozen tasks, Titus was in for a load of labor.

Titus was a Greek Christian, taught and nurtured by Paul. Like Timothy—another of Paul's spiritual sons—Titus was a close friend and fellow missionary of Paul's, eventually becoming the overseer of the churches on the island of Crete.

Paul's letter to Titus is a thorough explanation of the tasks of a church leader. What was Titus directed to do? First, he was told to deal with the leadership issue by choosing appropriate church leaders. Paul provided a list of qualifications these leaders needed.

Second, Titus was to rebuke those who refused to speak the truth. By this Paul referred to teachers who spread false doctrines and led people astray, as well as those who maligned the character of the people of Crete.

Third, Titus was expected to teach according to sound doctrine. Believers had to be grounded in the faith to avoid being swayed by false teaching, circumstances, stress, or emotions.

Fourth, fifth, and sixth, Titus was instructed in how to relate to the many different age groups within the church. "Teach the older men to be temperate, worthy of respect, self-controlled, and sound in faith, in love, and in endurance. Likewise, teach the older women to be reverent. . . . Similarly, encourage the young men to be self-controlled" (Titus 2:2–6 NIV).

For the seventh task, Paul told Titus to teach slaves to be subject to their masters, in order to make the teaching of the gospel "attractive" (2:10). He had the same advice for the slave Onesimus, as he described in his letter to Philemon.

Eighth, Titus had the authority to rebuke or encourage those under his charge. Paul spoke from experience.

Ninth, Titus was to remind the members of the body of Christ to be subject to those in authority. Christians then—and now—owed their allegiance first and foremost to Jesus Christ. But they were also to respect government leaders, employers, and others in authority over them.

Tenth, Titus was to keep reminding the people under his authority "to devote themselves to doing what is good" (3:8 NIV).

Eleventh, Paul warned Titus to avoid foolish controversies.

Although a discussion of doctrinal truths could lead to a deeper understanding of what it meant to be a Christian, Paul pointed out
that some discussions devolved into silly arguments.

And finally, Titus was told to visit Paul and provide for missionaries in need. While these tasks might seem laborious, they were a
labor of love to Titus. And Paul knew that Titus would not labor
alone—he had the Holy Spirit, who was always there to provide
supernatural guidance and strength a hero like Hercules could only
dream of.

*Read more details about these tough tasks in Titus 1–3.*

# PART SIX

# Dashers and Vixens

# "Esau" His Blessing Disappear

*Esau Loses His Birthright and Blessing to His Younger Brother*

Factoids: Esau
- *Domicile:* Canaan
- *Date:* Around 1900 B.C.
- *Occupation:* Hunter
- *Family Ties:* Parents, Isaac and Rebekah; brother, Jacob; wives: Judith, Basemath, and Mahalath
- *Mentioned in the Bible:* Genesis 25–36; Malachi 1:2–3; Romans 9:13; Hebrews 12:16–17

ESAU JUST COULDN'T catch a break. He was the elder son, but he was, from the very start, set to come in behind his brother! When Esau and his twin brother, Jacob, were in the womb, God told Rachel that even though Esau would be born first and technically be the elder brother, Jacob would become the head of the family in place of his older brother (see Genesis 25:23).

And that's exactly how the story played out.

Esau's father, Isaac, was getting along in years and was nearly blind. He decided he'd better give Esau, his firstborn, his blessing. (A father's blessing was a really big deal in Old Testament times, almost as if the blessing itself held supernatural power. A father bestowed a special blessing upon his firstborn son. The birthright also was to go to the eldest son, but if you remember, Esau had sold Jacob his birthright for a bowl of stew—read Genesis 25:27–34.)

In preparation of this blessing ceremony, Isaac told Esau to go hunting—he liked the taste of wild game—and said, "Prepare me the kind of tasty food I like and bring it to me to eat, so that I may give you my blessing before I die" (Genesis 27:4 NIV). Unfortunately, Rebekah overheard their conversation and she had other ideas.

Rebekah called to Jacob and related to him the exchange between Isaac and Esau. Then she told him her plan, which basically went like this:

> *Rebekah:* Go out to the flock and bring in two goats. I'll prepare them they way your dad likes, and you serve the meal to him. Then you'll get his blessing instead of Esau! Any questions?
> *Jacob:* Um, I don't think this is gonna work, Mom. Esau's really hairy and I'm not. If dad figures it out, he'll curse me instead of bless me.
> *Rebekah:* If he figures it out, the curse can fall on me! Just do as I say, boy.

What in the world was she thinking? Impatient and unwilling to trust God at his word, she had taken matters into her own hands.

Jacob did as he was told. Rebekah dressed him up in Esau's clothes so he'd smell like his brother and wrapped his arms and hands in goatskins so he'd feel like his brother (Esau must have been one hairy dude!). Then Jacob took the food she had prepared and served it to his dad.

Isaac knew something was suspicious. Even though Jacob smelled and felt like Esau, the voice was definitely Jacob's. When questioned by Isaac, Jacob perpetuated the lie. In the long run, he got what his mother wanted him to get: the blessing of the birthright.

When Esau then prepared the wild game and went to serve it to Isaac, what a surprise it must have been to both of them at the sad realization of what had taken place. In fact, the Bible tells us that "Isaac trembled violently" (27:33).

At the loss of his blessing and birthright, Esau was out for Jacob's blood. "Esau held a grudge against Jacob because of the blessing his father had given him. He said to himself, 'The days of mourning for my father are near; then I will kill my brother Jacob'" (27:41).

So Jacob ran for his life, ending up with his mother's relatives. Her brother, Laban, was just as full of tricks as Jacob. But that's another story. You can read about what happens when two tricksters meet up in the next story, "The Trickster Trailed."

*"Esau" his blessing disappear in Genesis 27.*

# The Trickster Trailed

*Jacob Is on the Run from His Uncle Laban*

Factoids: Jacob
- *Domicile:* Canaan
- *Date:* Around 1900 B.C.
- *Occupation:* Shepherd, livestock owner
- *Family Ties:* Parents, Isaac and Rebekah; brother, Esau; father-in-law, Laban; wives: Leah and Rachel; twelve

sons whose descendants became the twelve tribes of
Israel, and one daughter
- *Mentioned in the Bible:* Genesis 25–50; Exodus 3:6, 15–
  16; 6:2, 8; Hosea 12:2–5; Matthew 1:2; 22:32; Acts 3:13;
  7:46; Romans 9:11–13, 11:26; Hebrews 11:9, 20–21

JACOB WAS ON THE RUN. He had already stolen his older brother's
birthright and blessing (see the preceding story). For his own
safety, his mother had sent him packing, telling him, "Get ready and
flee to my brother, Laban, in Haran. Stay there with him until your
brother cools off " (Genesis 27:43–44 NLT).

While there, Jacob fell in love with Laban's daughter, Rachel,
and worked for seven years to pay the dowry for her hand in marriage. Yet on the wedding night, Laban snuck his older daughter,
Leah, into the ceremony in Rachel's place.

The next morning, when Jacob saw who lay next to him, he was
really ticked off. (The previous night must have been extremely
dark for him not to notice a different woman!) The trickster wasn't
thrilled when the tables were turned. "I worked seven years for
Rachel! Why have you tricked me?" Jacob raged at Laban (29:25).

Laban had simply heard opportunity knocking and had answered the door. His elder daughter wasn't much to look at, and
this was his only chance to marry her off. Besides, according to
custom, a younger daughter could not be married before the elder
one (a little detail he forgot to mention during those seven years).
Plus, if he got seven years' hard labor out of Jacob when he *thought*
he was working for Rachel, then surely he'd get another seven out
of him in order to *actually get* Rachel. And that's exactly what happened. Jacob finally got the woman of his dreams.

Eleven children later, Jacob heard from God: "Return to the
land of your father and grandfather and to your relatives there, and
I will be with you" (31:3).

Rather than tell Laban of his plans, Jacob decided to sneak
away . . . if one can make a quiet exit with two wives, eleven sons,

one daughter, and a host of servants, flocks, camels, and so forth. "Jacob outwitted Laban the Aramean, for they set out secretly and never told Laban they were leaving" (31:20).

Perhaps Rachel had learned a thing or two about deceit from her husband, or maybe she wanted to steal something of her father's. Whatever the reason, she "stole her father's household idols" (31:19) as the caravan fled to Gilead.

Laban may not have wanted to kill Jacob as Esau did, but he was upset enough to chase after him, even with Jacob's three-day head start. When Laban caught up to Jacob, their conversation went something like this:

> *Laban:* Whaddaya think you're doing, sneaking away with my daughters and grandkids? I could have thrown you a really nice bon voyage party, but, no-ooo. You didn't even let me say good-bye! And one more thing— why'd you steal my idols?
>
> *Jacob:* Hey, I thought you'd say no and force my wives to stay with you. I couldn't let that happen, now could I? Um, what idols?
>
> *Laban:* (deep sigh) Never mind. I'll just go look for them myself.

He never did find the idols. Rachel hid them, sat on top of them, and then said her "female problems" prevented her from getting up from her seat when Laban came looking. Laban finally went back home and Jacob continued on his way.

Jacob had learned a lesson or two about tricking people— mainly that it wasn't fun to be on the receiving end.

*To read about Jacob's tricky adventures, see Genesis 28–31.*

# Tempting Tamar

*Tamar Dresses as a Prostitute to Tempt Her Father-in-Law*

JUST READING the subtitle of this section makes the stomach queasy. Such an act is wrong on so many levels. But we should reserve judgment until we have the whole story.

Shortly after selling his little brother, Joseph, into slavery, Judah moved away from the family. He married a Canaanite woman and they had three sons together. Some years later the boys were getting to the age where Judah needed to find a wife for his eldest son, Er. He found a woman named Tamar. "But Er, Judah's firstborn, was wicked in the LORD's sight; so the LORD put him to death" (Genesis 38:7 NIV). Er died before Tamar conceived. Because Er had no son, there was no family line through which the firstborn inheritance could pass.

As was the law (see Deuteronomy 25:5–10), Er's younger brother Onan had to marry his brother's childless widow. (The first purpose of this law was to ensure that an heir would be produced to take the place of the firstborn, thus ensuring the passage of the all-important birthright. This system also ensured that there would be someone to care for the widow in later years.)

"Then Judah said to Onan, 'Lie with your brother's wife and fulfill your duty to her as a brother-in-law to produce offspring for your brother.' But Onan knew that the offspring would not be his; so whenever he lay with his brother's wife, he spilled his semen on the ground to keep from producing offspring for his brother" (Genesis 38:8–9). By acting so selfishly, Onan was denying Tamar any hope for the future, and breaking Hebrew law. "What he did was wicked in the LORD's sight; so he put him to death also" (38:10).

Tamar—a widow twice over—was probably starting to get a little paranoid. And Judah must have thought his daughter-in-law was cursed. He knew he had to give his third son to Tamar, but at this point, he was worried for the boy's well-being! So he said to Tamar, "Live as a widow in your father's house until my son Shelah grows up" (38:11). His comment held the promise that one day Shelah would take her as his wife, redeem her from the poverty of being a childless widow, and continue Judah's family line.

Many years passed and Tamar heard nothing from Judah.

It was obvious to her that Judah wasn't going to keep his end of the deal, so Tamar took matters into her own hands. She disguised herself as a prostitute, hid her face behind a veil, and sat on the road where she knew Judah would be traveling.

(We should note that prostitutes were common in Canaan and were often connected with religious cults. Tamar fell to the temptation to seduce Judah out of her desire to have children and continue the family line—pretending to be a prostitute was the easiest way to accomplish that goal. Judah fell to her seduction out of simple lust. God did not approve of this method, but in his infinite wisdom, worked it all out for a good ending.)

Judah saw her by the road and asked her to sleep with him.

"What will you give me?" she asked.

"I'll send a young goat from my flock," he said.

"I need some collateral," she replied. "How about giving me your seal and its cord, and the staff in your hand?" The seal was like the signet ring of a king—it served as identification for the owner. Now, because Tamar had possession of Judah's seal, she could prove that he was the man who caused her pregnancy. And that's exactly what happened.

When Judah tried to pay for his tryst and get his collateral back, the prostitute couldn't be found. Three months later, Tamar re-vealed she was pregnant. Judah, assuming Tamar was guilty of prostitution (which she was), said, "Bring her out and have her burned to death!" (38:24).

In an ironic twist that must have enraged and sickened Judah, Tamar sent a message saying she was pregnant by the owner of some specific items—a seal, a cord, and a staff. Judah recognized his belongings.

By not honoring his promise to Tamar, he had driven her to desperate measures. She became the matriarch of his bloodline, securing her hope for the future. As mentioned earlier, God turned this tragic situation into good for all mankind—Judah and Tamar are direct ancestors of Jesus Christ (see Matthew 1:1–3), making Tamar the first of only five women named in the bloodline of the Messiah.

*For all the details of the strange story of Tamar, read Genesis 38.*

# Dash from Danger

*Joseph Runs from Potiphar's Wife to Avoid Committing Adultery*

Factoids: Joseph
- *Domicile:* Canaan; Egypt
- *Date:* Around 1750 B.C.
- *Occupation:* Shepherd, slave, prisoner, ruler
- *Family Ties:* Parents, Jacob and Rachel; ten

brothers and one sister; wife, Asenath; sons, Manesseh and Ephraim

- *Mentioned in the Bible:* Genesis 30–50; Hebrews 11:22

P OOR JOSEPH had it tough from the start. Life began with ten older brothers who were jealous of the love and attention he received from their father. In fact, they hated Joseph so much they sold him into slavery, and then deceived their father, Jacob, about his demise (Genesis 37:12–35), proving once again that the apple doesn't fall far from the tree. (Jacob had sort of a deceiving streak himself. Read about that in "The Trickster Trailed," page 211.)

Joseph wound up with a caravan of Midianite traders on their way to Egypt. The strapping young man should fetch a good price. Sure enough, a prominent Egyptian named Potiphar bought Joseph, and although he was a slave, things started to go Joseph's way.

"When his master saw that the LORD was with him, and that the LORD gave him success in everything he did, Joseph found favor in his eyes and became his attendant. Potiphar put him in charge of his household and he entrusted to his care everything he owned" (Genesis 39:3–4 NIV). Potiphar was so impressed with Joseph's management skills, "he left in Joseph's care everything he had; with Joseph in charge, he did not concern himself with anything except the food he ate" (39:6).

Joseph was given the gift—or maybe the curse—of being well-built and handsome. Apparently being a good-looking guy four thousand years ago meant the same thing as it does today: ladies sit up and take notice.

In Joseph's case, the lady was Potiphar's wife. She was not especially concerned with her marriage vows and didn't waste time flirting. "Come to bed with me," she said (39:7), but Joseph refused.

Although the woman attempted to seduce him day after day, Joseph stood firm and told her, "My master has withheld nothing from me except you, because you are his wife. How then could I do such a wicked thing and sin against God?" (39:9). It seems that

Joseph had a conscience about sinning against God and betraying someone's trust. Could it be that he was different from the rest of his family?

Even though Joseph was turning out to be a man of integrity, Potiphar's wife couldn't stand being spurned any longer. When no one else was in the house, she grabbed him by the coat and once again said, "Come to bed with me!" (39:12), but he refused her one last time by running from the scene. Angry at being rebuffed, she made up a story to tell to her servants and Potiphar, which landed Joseph in prison. Even though Joseph was falsely accused, God blessed him for his willingness to stay pure and abide by his laws.

Sometimes saying no and avoiding temptation isn't enough. Sometimes it's best to just run away from a bad situation.

*The story of Joseph's dash from danger is in Genesis 39.*

# Moses, Murder, and Mayhem

*Moses Runs from Pharaoh After Murdering an Egyptian*

GROWING UP in Pharaoh's palace, Moses had it all. The adopted son of Pharaoh's daughter, he grew up in luxury with servants at his beck and call, was educated by the best minds in Egypt, and was trained for warfare by the most advanced army in the world. By every outward measure, Moses *was* an Egyptian prince, poised for leadership and authority.

Yet, it's evident from the brief account in Exodus 2:11–15 that, while Moses spent most of his growing-up years an "Egyptian," he had not forgotten his roots. His people were Hebrews, the slaves who labored daily to construct the roads, buildings, and monuments that made Egypt great. On this particular day, the young prince had gone to visit the laborers and was astounded by what he saw—his people, old and young alike, forced to toil in the hot sun, carrying heavy stones, making bricks from straw, with little or no rest or water. He could not believe how hard the people were forced to work.

As he was taking this in, he witnessed an Egyptian foreman beating one of the Hebrew slaves. Incensed, he quickly looked around. No one was watching. Moses killed the Egyptian and then buried him in the sand.

Thinking that he had—literally—gotten away with murder, Moses returned the next day to visit his people. This time, he spied two Hebrew men fighting with each other. Immediately, Moses relied on his princely authority to intervene and accosted the man who started it: "Why are you beating up your friend?" (Exodus 2:13 NLT).

The man was not intimidated by Moses's accusation. Boldly he stepped up to Moses and said, "Who appointed you to be our prince and judge? Are you going to kill me as you killed that Egyptian yesterday?" (2:14).

Busted! He *had* been seen, and it appeared that the entire Hebrew community knew what he had done. Badly shaken, Moses realized it would not be long before Pharaoh discovered what had happened and would arrest him.

Sure enough, Pharaoh did find out about the murder and ordered that Moses be arrested and killed. All the gold, the rich foods, the luxuries that Moses had enjoyed while living under Pharaoh's roof were meaningless now as Moses feared for his very life. What to do?

Moses took the only course of action he felt was open to him—he ran. Leaving behind his Hebrew roots as well as his Egyptian up-bringing, Moses fled as far as he could, across the Sinai desert to Midian. Finally, he stopped to rest by a well to get his bearings. He was alone, separated from everything and everyone he had ever known, a stranger in a strange land.

It would have been easy at this point in Moses's life for God to close the book on him. He had blown it. After all, he had killed an-other man (an Egyptian, no less), and he had abandoned his people, knowing full well their plight. He was a murderer, a marked man on the run. What use could God have for such a man?

Thankfully, the rest of the story is that God did use Moses, in powerful and amazing ways. It took years of living as a lowly shep-herd among the Midianites before Moses was ready to serve God again. But no matter how bleak or dark the future looked, Moses never gave up trusting that God would deliver him.

We shouldn't either, no matter what we may be running from.

*Moses's dash from Pharaoh is recorded in Exodus 2:11–25.*

# Delilah's Deception

*Delilah Deceives Samson*

N O LIST of Bible vixens would be complete without a reference to Delilah, the love of Samson's life, who was not above selling him out for a pile of money.

Samson fell in love with Delilah, who lived in the land of the Philistines in the Valley of Sorek. The Philistines had been enemies of the Israelites since the very earliest days of the kingdom, and Samson had his own history with the Philistines (read more about that in "A Strong Man's Weakness," page 177). When the Philistine leaders heard that Samson and Delilah were an item, they contacted Delilah and offered her an exorbitant amount of money to find out the secret to Samson's strength. Apparently, Delilah loved money more than she loved Samson, because she began trying to find out what made Samson so strong.

First, he told her that if he were tied up with "seven new bow-strings," he would lose his strength (Judges 16:7 NLT).

So she tied him up with seven new bowstrings.

It didn't work.

Then she put on her little pout, accused Samson of making fun of her, and asked again.

This time he told her that if he were tied up with brand-new, never-used ropes, he would lose his strength.

So she tied him up with brand-new, never-used ropes.

It didn't work.

So she pouted a little more. One wonders if she ever asked herself why Samson kept allowing her to try out the plan he had just given her. Maybe he really was a big dumb jock. In any case, she asked again.

This time he told her to weave his long hair into the fabric on her loom and tighten it with the shuttle. *Then* he would lose his strength.

She wove his hair into her loom.

It didn't work.

Now Delilah was getting a little bit ticked. Piles of money were riding on her finding out this secret. Maybe this stupid guy wasn't so stupid after all.

So she tried that secret weapon that females have known since the beginning of time: nagging. She nagged Samson so much that he finally gave in and told her that cutting his hair would cause him to lose his strength.

So she cut his hair.

It worked!

Were there any parting words between Samson and Delilah? Did Delilah ever feel any guilt for what she did? Or did having so much money overshadow the guilt? Delilah's deceit raises more questions than we can answer. We don't always remember the name of the person who brought down a public figure, but we always hear Delilah's name in conjunction with Samson's. Delilah left a legacy of deceit, manipulation, and the love of money.

Oh yeah, and the power of nagging.

*Delilah's deception is recorded in Judges 16.*

# Only Fools Rush In

*Saul Hurriedly Offers a Sacrifice and Loses His Crown over It*

Factoids: Saul
- *Domicile:* Land of Benjamin
- *Date:* Around 1045 B.C.
- *Occupation:* King
- *Family Ties:* Father, Kish; sons, Jonathan and Ish-Bosheth; wife, Ahinoam; daughters, Merab and Michal
- *Mentioned in the Bible:* 1 Samuel 9–31; Acts 13:21

SAMUEL WAS the last judge of Israel. He decided to retire when he heard grumblings from the Israelites that they no longer wanted a judge to be in charge. Instead, they wanted what every other nation in the lands surrounding them had: a king—a real flesh-and-blood, crown-wearing, throne-sitting king. Samuel tried to talk them out of the idea, but as was the recurring theme of the Old Testament, the people didn't listen to wise counsel. So God told Samuel to anoint Saul as Israel's first king. (See more in "A Royal Pain," page 122.)

Saul, only thirty years old when he became king, was a proficient soldier and skillful military leader, but he never matured much past the arrogance of youth.

Saul's kingdom was often faced with warfare, and the nation of Philistia, to the southwest by the sea, was a constant enemy. At one point Saul's son, Jonathan, attacked a Philistine outpost and won, but Saul took all the credit (see 1 Samuel 13:3–4).

The victory only caused more trouble. Enraged that their outpost had been destroyed, "the Philistines assembled to fight Israel, with three thousand chariots, six thousand charioteers, and soldiers as numerous as the sand on the seashore. They went up and camped at Micmash, east of Beth Aven. When the men of Israel saw that their situation was critical and that their army was hard pressed, they hid in caves and thickets, among the rocks, and in pits and cisterns" (13:5–6 NIV).

Apparently, Saul and the Israelites forgot that God was on their side.

Saul watched as his army began to melt with fear. He knew that if he continued to wait, the army would completely lose heart (if not disappear), and defeat would be imminent. Saul wanted to perform a sacrifice and pray before going into battle—and he needed the priest, Samuel, to do that. Samuel had directed Saul to wait seven days. On the seventh day, Samuel would offer up a sacrifice to God.

But, out of impatience and under pressure from the approaching Philistines, Saul brazenly offered up the sacrifice on his own, something expressly forbidden by God's law. As he finished making the offering, Samuel arrived. "What have you done?" he asked.

Saul had plenty of excuses for his disobedience: "My men were scattering . . . you were late . . . the Philistines were closing in . . . I felt compelled to offer the burnt offering . . ." (13:11–12).

Samuel had a way of zeroing in on the issue. "You acted foolishly. You have not kept the command the LORD your God gave you" (13:13). It wasn't what he did (seeking the Lord's favor with an offering) but how he did it (only the priest was to offer the burnt offering). This was brazen disobedience—something that had become Saul's modus operandi.

This should have been a no-brainer. Saul thought he would hurry along the victory for his kingdom but ended up cursing his own monarchy. Because of his rash decision, neither his son—nor any of his direct descendants—would sit upon the throne of Israel. *For the story about Saul's hurried and inappropriate actions, read 1 Samuel 13.*

# Band on the Run

*David Amasses a Group of Fighting Men and Spends Years Running from Saul*

FOR MORE THAN a hundred nail-biting episodes, actor David Janssen as Dr. Richard Kimble was on the run in the popular 1960s television series *The Fugitive.* Falsely accused and convicted of murdering his wife, Kimble spent each episode one step ahead of the law, trying to prove his innocence before the FBI could capture and throw him in prison.

*The Fugitive* could have been modeled after David's life. Like Dr. Richard Kimble, David was a man on the run. Like Kimble, David was falsely accused and hunted down. But unlike Kimble, whose years on the run were solitary and friendless, David had a faithful and loyal following of men.

Hiding in the cave of Adullam, David sought refuge from the murderous King Saul. David had incurred the jealous king's wrath because he had secured more victories in the field against Israel's enemies than Saul had, and also because God had anointed David the next king, instead of Saul's son, Jonathan. For these "crimes,"

Saul had vowed to kill David and had enlisted the entire army of Israel to help him accomplish his goals.

At first David's brothers and other family members joined the exiled David. Then, as word spread, more men began coming. In all, four hundred made their way to David's side. It was a ragtag assortment of misfits, outcasts, and those who were in trouble, in debt, or simply discontented with their lot in life. In David they saw hope for a new life with a new king.

Though he was on the run from Saul and Israel's army, David could not stand by as Israel's enemies warred against his countrymen. When he heard that the hated Philistines were raiding the town of Keilah, David led his men on a daring attack and slaughtered the enemy. In victory David and his men still were not safe from Saul's wrath. Hearing that David and his men were in the walled city of Keilah, Saul was certain he had David trapped. Hot on the trail, Saul headed for Keilah—but not before David learned of Saul's intent and escaped with his men into the wilderness.

Roaming the countryside, David's ranks had now swelled to six hundred men. Day by day Saul relentlessly hunted David. But God didn't let him find David. Even when the men of Ziph betrayed David and told Saul where to find him, David and his men were able to escape into the stronghold of En-gedi, a wildness filled with caves and places to hide.

Not to be deterred, Saul selected three thousand special troops and headed into the En-gedi hills to track down his nemesis. Twice while in pursuit, Saul was placed within David's grasp. Twice, David easily could have killed his sworn enemy and found relief from the tyranny of the hunt. Repeatedly, David's men pleaded with him to kill Saul and take his rightful place as king. But David was resolute in his belief that God had anointed Saul and placed him on the throne. In God's timing—not his—David, too, would be named king of Israel.

David finally sought refuge with the enemy, under the protection of the Philistine king Achish. When Saul discovered this, he gave up the chase because his army was not strong enough to invade enemy territory to hunt down one man. Even then David and his men continued their attacks on the Philistines, conducting clandestine raids against the border tribes and deceiving the Philistine king into thinking that they were attacking their own countrymen.

Eventually, Saul was severely wounded in battle against the Philistines. Rather than be captured and tortured by his lifelong enemies, Saul took his own life. When David heard the news, he wept and mourned the man who had hunted him down for all those long years. At long last the time had come, and David took his rightful place on the throne.

As for his faithful band of men? Under David's leadership, with skills honed by years on the run, this loyal assortment of misfits and rebels became the core of his military leadership and the foundation of David's renowned "mighty men" (2 Samuel 23:8).

*To find out more about David and his band of misfits on the run, read 1 Samuel 19–29.*

# A Hairy Situation

*Absalom Winds Up on the Run After Trying to Take His Father's Kingdom*

Factoids: Absalom
- *Domicile:* Hebron
- *Date:* Around 985 B.C.
- *Occupation:* Prince
- *Family Ties:* Father, David; mother, Maacah; brothers, Amnon, Kileab, Solomon, and others; sister, Tamar
- *Mentioned in the Bible:* 2 Samuel 3:3 and 13–19

ABSALOM KNEW HOW to run. Early on he ran from his father's guidance and authority. As a murderer he ran to a city of refuge from those who would bring him to justice. In the heat of battle he ran to save his life. Worst of all, because of his refusal to repent, he ran from God.

Absalom was King David's son, third in line for the throne. We are told that he was very attractive: "No one in all Israel was as handsome and well-built as Absalom. He got his hair cut once a year, and when the hair was weighed, it came to about five pounds" (2 Samuel 14:25–26 CEV).

But, in spite of his looks, he had a dark side.

When his eldest half brother, Amnon, raped Absalom's sister, Tamar, Absalom was furious. Yet he contained his fury for two long years, during which time he plotted his revenge. When the time was right, he ordered his men to kill Amnon (see 2 Samuel 13:28).

Then, to avoid punishment for his deed, "Absalom [ran] away to Geshur, where he stayed for three years with King Talmai the son of Ammihud" (13:37–38).

Through a bit of plotting and subterfuge, Absalom was granted amnesty for his deeds and was allowed to return to his house in Jerusalem. While there his conspiracy against his father began. His political strategy would have rivaled that of some of the best politicians of today. He set out to win the hearts and minds of the people, while simultaneously turning them against David. Daily he would sit at the city gate and speak to all who entered. "Whenever anyone would come to Absalom and start bowing down, he would reach out and hug and kiss them. That's how he treated everyone from Israel who brought a complaint to the king. Soon everyone in Israel liked Absalom better than they liked David" (15:5–6).

Absalom's good looks, friendliness, and seeming concern for the people fueled the full-scale rebellion which sent David into retreat from the palace (read about that in "Curse for a King," page 48). David realized how widespread the uprising had become and chose to flee rather than put his family or innocent citizens in harm's way. However, he wisely sent a spy, Hushai, to thwart Absalom's adviser and report back to him.

Unaware of the allegiance of Hushai, Absalom took the spy's advice over that of the adviser. Also unaware that his father knew he was coming, Absalom gathered a huge army and went in pursuit of the king. When his army was routed on the battlefield, Absalom fled for the final time. He rode his donkey into a thicket in order to hide and "his head caught in the branches. The mule ran off and left Absalom hanging in midair" (18:9).

Although David told his officers not to harm Absalom, Joab, David's general, killed Absalom as he hung there helplessly by his beautiful thick hair.

A hairy situation that proved to be his undoing.

*To read the story of Absalom's turbulent life, see 2 Samuel 13–18.*

# Led Astray

*Solomon's Wives Lead Him away from God*

THERE AREN'T a whole lot of places in Scripture where God prescribes who people can and can't marry. But in Solomon's case, the Lord had told his people in no uncertain terms, "You must not intermarry with them [Moabites, Ammonites, Edomites, Sidonians, and Hittites], because they will surely turn your hearts after their gods" (1 Kings 11:2 NIV).

Sounds pretty clear.

Yet Solomon chose to disregard God's command, setting a poor example for the entire nation. He married not one but many idolatrous women: "He had seven hundred wives of royal birth and three hundred concubines, and his wives led him astray. As Solomon grew old, his wives turned his heart after other gods, and his heart was not fully devoted to the LORD his God, as the heart of David his father had been" (11:3–4).

Solomon was the wisest king of Israel, and quite possibly the wisest human being ever to have walked the earth. Yet in spite of his wisdom, he had weaknesses and fell to temptation, just as every one of us has done. Solomon compromised his faith in God in order to please his wives—and he had a lot of wives to keep happy! In fact, he built each one of them their own little "high place" where he could burn incense and offer sacrifices to their gods (see 11:7–8).

He probably justified his marriages—all seven hundred of them—as necessary to strengthen political alliances. But he was clearly going against God's plan for him, one marriage after another, over many years. And the consequences were rather unpleasant.

> The LORD became angry with Solomon because his heart had turned away from the LORD, the God of Israel, who had appeared to him twice. Although he had forbidden Solomon to follow other gods, Solomon did not keep the LORD's command. So the LORD said to Solomon, "Since this is your attitude and you have not kept my covenant and my decrees, which I commanded you, I will most certainly tear the kingdom away from you and give it to one of your subordinates. Nevertheless, for the sake of David your father, I will not do it during your lifetime. I will tear it out of the hand of your son." (1 Kings 11:9–12)

Solomon's kingdom could have been blessed for a long time, and could have been passed in its entirety to his son and on down through the generations. What began as sinfully ignoring God's command became the continual weakening of Solomon's faith, resulting in his own downfall and the ultimate division of the kingdom. (For that full story, read "A 'Tear'-ible Thing" on page 125.)

*To read about Solomon's wives, their many gods, and how they led Solomon astray, see 1 Kings 11.*

# Dashing from
# the Vixen

*Elijah Dashes Past Ahab's Chariot—and from the Vixen
Jezebel*

Factoids: Jezebel
- *Domicile:* From Sidon, then lived in the palace in Samaria, capital of the northern kingdom of Israel
- *Date:* Around 870 B.C.
- *Occupation:* Queen of the northern kingdom of Israel
- *Family Ties:* Father, Ethbaal; husband, Ahab; sons, Ahaziah, Joram
- *Mentioned in the Bible:* 1 Kings 16:31–2 Kings 9:37. Her name is used as a synonym for evil in Revelation 2:20.

T HE MOST FAMOUS of Israel's prophets, Elijah, was not known for his athletic ability or physical strength.

Instead he was known for the dramatic way in which he presented God's word to the people of Israel, and to their king, Ahab. However, immediately following one of the more spectacular displays of God's power, Elijah was given supernatural strength and endurance for an amazing race.

Here's the backstory: King Ahab and his evil wife, Jezebel, had attempted to kill off all of the prophets of God. For this reason, and because Ahab and Jezebel were idol worshippers, the land had been struck with severe drought and famine. God told Elijah to go and present himself to Ahab, and then he would send rain.

When Ahab saw Elijah, he called out, "Is it you, you troubler of Israel?" (1 Kings 18:17 ESV).

Elijah replied to this insult by reminding Ahab that it was the king's fault that Israel was in dire straits. "I have not troubled Israel, but you have, and your father's house, because you have abandoned the commandments of the LORD and followed the Baals [popular Canaanite gods]" (18:18). Elijah then instructed Ahab to summon all the people of Israel to meet him on Mount Carmel. Elijah told Ahab also to bring along with him the 450 prophets of Baal, and Jezebel's 400 prophets of Asherah.

Once there Elijah began preaching. His sermon concluded with these words: "How long will you go limping between two different opinions? If the LORD is God, follow him; but if Baal, then follow him" (18:21).

Then a contest began—the god who sent fire would be declared the winner. Two altars were built and two bulls sacrificed—one to the Lord God, and one to Baal. The prophets of Baal cried out, danced, and even slashed themselves with swords. They did this all day long, to no avail. Then it was Elijah's turn. After a simple prayer the Lord answered with fire from heaven, which consumed the sacrifice. "And when all the people saw it, they fell on their faces and said, 'The LORD, he is God; the LORD, he is God'" (18:39). Then the people of Israel killed all of the false prophets.

The Lord promised to answer his people's return to him by giving them the rain they so desperately needed. Elijah knew the rain was coming. From the mountainside he told his servant to look toward the sea. Finally, the servant reported seeing a cloud as small as a man's hand. Elijah knew the rain was coming quickly, so he sent Ahab back to Jezreel before the rain could stop him. Then "the hand of the LORD was on Elijah, and he gathered up his garment and ran before Ahab to the entrance of Jezreel" (18:46). Imagine

Ahab's astonishment as this prophet outran his horse and chariot for the six miles back to the city!

When Ahab returned, he recounted to Jezebel the day's events on the mountain, including the slaughter of the false prophets. Enraged that her yes-men were all dead, Jezebel pledged to kill Elijah.

So Elijah started running again—but this time far, far away from the vixen queen. This may seem an odd reaction from one who had just witnessed the power of God on the mountain and then received the supernatural power to outrun the king's chariot. But Elijah knew that even though the people of Israel repented and proclaimed the Lord is God, Jezebel's heart was hardened past the point of repentance.

And Elijah was tired. Sometimes after a great victory (and a run of several miles!), even the most powerful prophet needs a little R&R. God gave it to his servant, and then sent him back to work.

*To read the story of Elijah and his fleet-footed flights, see 1 Kings 18:44–19:3.*

# A Not-So-Great Grandma

*Joash Barely Survives the Death Plot of His Grandmother, Athaliah*

Factoids: Joash
- *Domicile:* Jerusalem
- *Date:* Around 835 B.C.
- *Occupation:* King
- *Family Ties:* Father, Ahaziah; mother, Zibiah; grandmother, Athaliah; son, Amaziah; aunt, Jehosheba; uncle, Jehoiada; cousin, Zechariah
- *Mentioned in the Bible:* 2 Kings 11–12; 2 Chronicles 22:10–24:27

ALL PARENTS WANT the best for their children, and most grandparents lovingly spoil their grandchildren. But in Joash's family, his sweet old grandma wasn't interested in pinching his cheeks or showering him with presents.

She wanted him dead.

Ahaziah had been king of Judah and passed away from wounds of battle. "When Athaliah the mother of Ahaziah saw that her son was dead, she proceeded to destroy the whole royal family" (2 Kings 11:1 NIV). Why did she do such an awful thing? To get rid of any competition. As the matriarch of a royal line, if she was the only one surviving, then she would take the throne and rule. She had a lust for power, and nothing—not even her grandchildren—could stand in her way.

Ahaziah's sister had other ideas. "But Jehosheba . . . took Joash son of Ahaziah and stole him away from among the royal princes, who were about to be murdered. She put him and his nurse in a bedroom to hide him from Athaliah; so he was not killed. He remained hidden with his nurse at the temple of the LORD for six years while Athaliah ruled the land" ( 2 Kings 11:2–3).

Jehosheba was the wife of the high priest Jehoiada. Knowing she couldn't save all the children, she had to make a difficult choice and saved only Joash. It made sense for her to hide and raise Joash in the temple. Athaliah was a worshipper of Baal and most likely kept her distance from the temple of the Lord. Also, she may not have been aware that any of her descendants had survived, and if she was, the temple of the Lord was the last place she would look.

Joash's aunt and uncle raised him in the temple while Athaliah ruled until Joash was seven years old. At that point Jehoiada arranged for the overthrow of the wicked grandmother and the crowning of the child as king. He hired mercenary troops (11:4–11) to protect Joash until he was anointed king of Judah. When the time was right, "Jehoiada brought out the king's son and put the crown on him; he presented him with a copy of the covenant and proclaimed him king. They anointed him and the people clapped their hands and shouted, 'Long live the king!'" (11:12).

When Athaliah heard the shouts of the people, she went out to find the cause of the hubbub. When she saw the boy who had been crowned as king, she tore her royal robes and cried out, "Treason! Treason!" (11:14). Having made herself conspicuous in an unfriendly crowd, she was seized and put to death.

Then the people promised (again) to be the Lord's people. They tore down the temple to Baal and killed the priest there.

Athaliah is a shocking example of the corruption of power. Nothing she could have done to end her son's family line would have succeeded, because God had promised that the Messiah would be born through the family line of David (see 2 Samuel 7). Athaliah wiped out everyone in that line—except Joash, thanks to the faithful protection of Jehoiada and Jehosheba.

*To read about this murderous grandmother, see 2 Kings 11:1–16.*

# The Dance of Death

*Two Vixens, a Dance, a Weak King, and a Grisly Death*

Factoids: Herod the Great
- *Domicile:* Judea
- *Date:* Ruled from 37–4 B.C.
- *Occupation:* King of the region of Judea
- *Family Ties:* Father, Antipater; sons, Archelaus, Antipater, Antipas, Philip, and others; wives, Mariamne, Doris, others
- *Mentioned in the Bible:* Matthew 2:1–22; Luke 1:5

SOME BIRTHDAY PARTY! What kind of girl would ask for a man's head on a platter when she had her choice of anything in the kingdom? Here's how it happened.

Herod Antipas was one of the four rulers of Palestine (hence the title "tetrarch"). He was an immoral man who took Herodias to be his wife. The problem with this situation was that Herodias was already the wife of Herod's brother, Philip, and Philip wasn't dead. But Herodias left her husband for her husband's brother, and John the Baptist criticized their relationship.

John the Baptist, not known for tact, made Herod's sinful relationship with Herodias a public issue. It was no secret that John condemned the tetrarch's adulterous marriage. Naturally, Herodias hated him. And King Herod wanted him silenced—for good. "Herod wanted to kill John, but he was afraid of the people, because they considered him a prophet" (Matthew 14:5 NIV). So he threw him in prison. That was easy.

On the night of Herod's birthday, Herodias's daughter presented her gift: a sultry dance. Although she is not named in Scripture, other documents name her as Salome. She must have been some dancer, because Herod was so dazzled that "he promised with an oath to give her whatever she asked" (14:6–7). Considering the wealth and power of Herod, Salome could have been set for life with this one gift. Unfortunately, she listened to the counsel of her mother. "Prompted by her mother, she said, 'Give me here on a platter the head of John the Baptist'" (14:8).

With a mother like that, who needs enemies?

Imagine the look of horror on each of the party guests' faces, the murmuring in disbelief. "What did she just say? Did she really ask for a man's head on a platter? What's she gonna do with that?"

Her request disturbed Herod. Suddenly the dangers of giving Salome carte blanche ("You can have anything, just name it") were crystal clear. Aside from the fact that Herod feared the reaction of the people for such an act, deep down he liked John the Baptist. After all, this was the only man who was willing to speak the truth to him, no matter how painful.

But the king's reputation was at stake. He had made an oath and he didn't want to be embarrassed in front of his guests. So he ordered the immediate beheading of John in prison.

Eventually the servants came in with the prize. "His head was brought in on a platter and given to the girl, who carried it to her mother" (14:11). Perhaps Salome did one more distracting dance. Perhaps her wicked mother drank a toast to her obliging husband. Meanwhile John's close friends came quietly, took his body, and buried it.

*To read about Salome's strange choice, read Matthew 14:1–12.*

# The First Streaker

*Mark Runs Naked Through the Garden After Jesus Is Arrested*

Factoids: John Mark
- *Domicile:* Jerusalem
- *Date:* Around A.D. 30
- *Occupation:* Follower of Jesus, Gospel writer, missionary
- *Family Ties:* Mother, Mary; cousin, Barnabas
- *Mentioned in the Bible:* Acts 12:25–13:13; 15:36–39; Colossians 4:10; 2 Timothy 4:11; Philemon 24; 1 Peter 5:13. He is referred to, although not by name, in Mark 14:51–52.

YOUR FIRST REACTION might be, "They're kidding, right? A streaker in the Bible?" Not only is this not a joke, but this event occurred during one of the most intense scenes in the New Testament—the arrest of Jesus in the Garden of Gethsemane.

The disciples had gone to the garden with Jesus after the Passover meal, which turned out to be the Last Supper. While Jesus was praying, the disciples all fell asleep. Knowing that his arrest would come soon, Jesus awakened the men just prior to the arrival of the betrayer, Judas Iscariot, and a group of soldiers.

Not comprehending the events that were unfolding, the disciples must have been greatly distressed when they woke up and saw soldiers seizing and arresting Jesus. Peter was so angry at the midnight posse that he drew his sword and cut off the ear of the servant of the high priest.

Luke 22:51 tells us that Jesus immediately healed the young man's ear. Perhaps Peter was aiming for the high priest and the servant jumped up to save his master. Regardless of the intentions, it is evident that the scene was a chaotic blend of men running, swords flashing, and a miracle healing.

Afraid they would also be arrested, the disciples all fled from the garden. Yet one man, the writer of this Gospel, was almost caught: "One young man following behind was clothed only in a long linen shirt. When the mob tried to grab him, he slipped out of his shirt and ran away naked" (Mark 14:51–52 NLT). Most scholars agree that the story is included here (and only in Mark's Gospel) as a bit of autobiography. Mark fled in such great fear that he literally leapt right out of his clothes! He wanted to do the right thing and stay with Jesus, but his basic survival instinct told him to run.

Although Scripture doesn't tell us how the soldiers reacted to this situation, we can guess that they laughed heartily as they watched his little white behind disappear among the olive trees. They may even have teased the soldier who tried to apprehend Mark and succeeded only in arresting an empty garment.

*To read about the mysterious garden streaker, see Mark 14:51–52.*

# A Loose Woman

*A Samaritan Woman Meets the Savior*

THERE ARE SOME parts of town people go out of their way to avoid: bad neighborhoods and seedy streets. In Jesus' day, people traveled miles out of their way to avoid the area of Samaria, not because of the crime-ridden streets but because of the people.

The Samaritans were related to the Jews but were considered half-breeds. One day, Jesus took his band of men on a detour into a Samaritan town. While the disciples went in search of food, a tired and thirsty Jesus waited at a well.

A Samaritan woman ventured to the well for water. Little did she know that the Doctor of Hearts was ready to see her.

Although the Gospel of John does not provide many details about this woman, there are some facts to be gleaned from her appearance. The fact that she was alone at the well at high noon showed her probable position in society. Many people collected their water later in the day, but there she was at noon with a water jar to be filled. She was probably well acquainted with the bottom rung of society.

"Give me a drink," Jesus said (John 4:7 ESV). While that statement might not sound shocking, it was to the woman at the well. A Jewish man would hardly have spoken to a strange woman of his own people, let alone a Samaritan woman. But she was not one for saying, "Mind your own business." Instead, she reminded Jesus of the cultural chasm between their people.

But Jesus would not be put off. He replied, "If you knew the gift of God, and who it is that is saying to you, 'Give me a drink,' you would have asked him, and he would have given you living water" (John 4:10).

Well, the Samaritan woman was not one to debate the merits of Aquafina versus Evian. Seeing as how she had no idea what living water was, she relied on practicalities: This well is deep and you, Jesus, have nothing with which to draw your alleged living water.

But Jesus would not be swayed by unimportant issues like that. If she drank his water, he assured her, she would never thirst again. This living water was eternal life.

When the woman readily agreed to try this living water, Jesus made an unusual request—she was to bring her husband to the well.

At this point the woman could have walked away, but she didn't. There was something unusual about Jesus, something that caused her to be honest instead of flippant. "I have no husband," she announced (4:17).

Now we get to the heart of the matter. She was a woman of loose morals, someone the "decent" women probably shunned.

Jesus wasn't shocked by her admission, knowing that she had had five husbands. By his response, she discerned that he was a prophet. But he wanted her to go beyond that distinction to one that was truer: he was the Messiah. Those who worshipped him, worshipped him with the spirit and in truth.

Although his disciples returned to the well stunned that Jesus spoke to the woman, she left the well determined to spread the good news. The Messiah had come! Best of all, he came for people like her—the broken and the believing.

*To read more about this living-water-drenched woman, see John 4.*

# Caught in the Act

*A Woman Is Arrested for Committing Adultery*

ALTHOUGH THE WOMAN in this account was caught in an act of sin, she was most definitely an innocent party in the Pharisees' attempt to trap Jesus with his own words. But as a result, this sinful woman came face-to-face with the Messiah.

One day while Jesus was teaching the crowds in the temple courts, "the teachers of the law and the Pharisees brought in a woman caught in adultery" (John 8:3 NIV). But these men who seemed so concerned about the law were disregarding it themselves—they had arrested only one of the guilty parties, and adultery takes two people. They brought only the woman to Jesus, suggesting that she had been lured into the relationship for the sole purpose of trapping her partners.

"They made her stand before the group and said to Jesus, 'Teacher, this woman was caught in the act of adultery. In the law, Moses commanded us to stone such women. Now what do you say?'" (8:3–5). In their eyes, Jesus could have no right answer. If he said, "Stone her," then they could report him to the Roman authorities, who didn't allow Jews to carry out executions. If Jesus said they should let her go, then he would be guilty of violating the law of Moses.

While the woman stood by, fully expecting death to come quickly, Jesus stooped and wrote on the ground with his finger. The Bible doesn't tell us what he wrote, or if the woman was close enough to read it.

He may have been listing the sins of the accusers.

Regardless of the message, they kept questioning Jesus until he stood up and said to them, "If any one of you is without sin, let him be the first to throw a stone at her" (John 8:7).

Evidently the older men in the group were more aware of their sins than the younger men. As they slipped quietly away, one by one, the older ones first, the woman's sense of dread must have changed to confusion.

She had been so close to death—what would happen to her now?

Then the Master turned to her and asked, "Woman, where are they? Has no one condemned you?"

"No one, sir," she said.

"Then neither do I condemn you," Jesus declared. "Go now and leave your life of sin" (8:10–11). With those words the woman received forgiveness. Jesus did not condone her sin but, rather, told her to change her ways, to turn over a new leaf.

*To read this account of the sinful woman who was forgiven instead of stoned, see John 8:1–11.*

# A Runaway Slave

*Onesimus Runs Away and Then Must Return*

Factoids: Onesimus
- *Domicile:* Colosse
- *Date:* About A.D. 60
- *Occupation:* Slave in Philemon's household
- *Family Ties:* Unknown
- *Mentioned in the Bible:* Colossians 4:9; the book of Philemon

ONESIMUS HAD SIGNED his own death warrant the moment he stepped foot outside Philemon's door. One of the millions of slaves living in the Roman empire, Onesimus had the dubious distinction not only of stealing from his wealthy master but also of running away. Either offense would have warranted punishment by death.

Onesimus was a doomed man.

That is, until he met Paul.

Onesimus ran away from Colosse, where his master lived, to Rome, the center of the empire. A man could get lost there, and that's what Onesimus hoped for. In what can only be described as divine intervention, he crossed paths with Paul, who at the time was under house arrest in Rome. (Perhaps Onesimus had been caught and thrown into prison as well? We don't know.) Through Paul's influence, Onesimus became a believer and a brother in Christ.

Here's where the story takes another divinely ordained twist, for it became apparent that Onesimus's master was none other than Philemon. Philemon was one of Paul's beloved coworkers from Colosse, and a man whom Paul had led to faith in Jesus Christ. In perhaps his most personal letter, Paul appealed to his brother-in-Christ's generous spirit to forgive his wayward slave.

Paul convinced Onesimus that running from his problems wouldn't make them go away, and he persuaded the slave that he needed to return to his master. Onesimus agreed without knowing what he might face upon his return. But what Onesimus did have was Paul's beautifully worded appeal to Philemon, not only to forgive his slave but also to be reconciled with his slave as a fellow believer and brother in Christ. "I appeal to you for my son Onesimus, who became my son while I was in chains. Formerly he was useless to you, but now he has become useful both to you and to me. I am sending him—who is my very heart—back to you," wrote Paul (Philemon 10–12 NIV).

Paul further showed his love for Onesimus by promising to pay for any damages or stolen goods that the slave might have been responsible for. If Philemon had any doubt of Paul's sincerity, this certainly would have erased any from his mind. Paul was clear in his desire that Onesimus be regarded and loved as a brother in Christ: "He is no longer just a slave; he is a beloved brother, especially to me. Now he will mean much more to you, both as a slave and as a brother in the Lord" (16).

The end of the story is not known, but we do have one clue as to how it all might have turned out. Some scholars believe this Onesimus is Onesimus *the bishop* who is praised in a letter to the second-century church at Ephesus from Ignatius of Antioch.

From slave to bishop? Only God could have orchestrated that.

*The story of the runaway slave Onesimus is recorded in the little book of Philemon.*

# Index

Printed in the United States
By Bookmasters